# Making Sense of the Economy

To Joseph

# Making Sense of the Economy

## Dominick Harrod

MARTIN ROBERTSON · OXFORD

© Dominick Harrod, 1983

First published in 1983 by
Martin Robertson & Company Ltd,
108 Cowley Road, Oxford OX4 1JF.

*British Library Cataloguing in Publication Data*

Harrod, Dominick
  Making sense of the economy.
  1. Great Britain – Economic conditions – 1945–
  1. Title
  330·941′0858        HC256.6

ISBN 0 85520 555 5
     0 85520 556 3 pbk

Typeset by Oxford Verbatim Limited
Printed and bound in Great Britain by
Billing and Sons Ltd, Worcester

# Contents

# Introduction

There is no subject in ordinary life which is anything like so fiercely argued over as the state of the economy. At every level, from a full-dress House of Commons debate on unemployment, to the argument in the local pub, the ever-interesting topics of inflation, taxation, public spending, borrowing, interest rates and the like rattle through the conversations, pompous or heated, and all turning on the two main questions about which few can ever agree: are things getting better or worse, and what's to be done about it?

In a long experience of writing and broadcasting about economics I've found that most of those who do the talking about economics fall into one of two classes: those who know nothing of economics and those who know it all! How often have I heard this statement (or something like it): 'Whenever the word "economics" is mentioned my mind switches off.' But even more numerous are the people who say – or, worse, write at length – that they have long perceived the secret of solving all our economic problems: if only the Government (or the trade unions, or the Bank of England, or just 'they') would take some simple step like abolishing income tax or returning to the Gold Standard, all would be well.

In the real world both the ignorant and the knowing are wide of the mark. People who protest that they know nothing of economics have just as profound an effect on the performance of the economy as the many people, from academics to businessmen and politicians, whose views of the economy and whose decisions about it are reckoned by themselves and by the rest of us watching them to be significant or even crucial.

In truth, the performance of the economy depends on the sum of all the decisions made by all the members of the economy – and in a country the size of Britain these run into literally millions every day. By far the greater number are made by people who know nothing of economics, nor wish to. You do not have to know how the internal combustion engine works to be able to drive a car, nor how a nuclear reactor generates electricity in order to turn on the light. But it is the hundreds of thousands of individuals in any community who easily, unthinkingly, add to or detract from its prosperity and success by their individual economic decisions.

There are also, of course, other kinds of decision which have altogether more emphatic consequences; a man or woman can, by one decision, affect the lives of many, many other people. For convenience, the types of decision made in the normal course of events, which deliberately or otherwise are of economic significance, may be grouped in three classes.

The first class is by far the largest and, as may emerge, also pretty important in the scheme of things, although the impact of such decisions on other individuals is relatively slight. These decisions, such as whether to take a holiday abroad or trade in the car a year earlier, are the personal decisions which affect the climate of the economy enormously. They cover a wide field – not only the sort of spending option just suggested but also such matters as savings (the choice between National Savings, a building society or shares on the Stock Exchange) and broader family decisions about education, work, medical insurance and even careers for the future. There are many who tell us that the weakness of the British economy is the product of an ingrained distaste for industry as compared with the liberal arts. If so, the decision taken by talented people not to seek satisfaction in certain sorts of job may have major economic importance, even though it is taken for entirely non-economic reasons.

The second large group of economic decisions taken every day or every year is what might be called 'corporate decisions'. These are mostly taken by employers rather than employees, by sellers rather than by buyers (though most of the concerns making such decisions are buyers too, who hope also to sell). They are decisions taken by every responsible manager from the owner of the small family business – be it a farm, or corner shop, a light industrial process employing three men and a boy – up to the executives of the giants of the corporate sector, the great public companies and the nationalized industries and state concerns, from British Airways to the Coal Board. And beyond them there are the non-commercial corporate bodies: the area health authorities and the education authorities, which have to decide not only on budgets for school textbooks but also how many teachers, and therefore how many places at teacher training colleges, they will need in coming years.

These corporate decisions, whether they are made by giant private companies like ICI or Shell or by public bodies like the British Railways Board or the Inner London Education Authority, border in importance on a third and quite distinct kind of decision-making, which affects the whole economic environment: that of government and its agents, both national and international.

Ever since I have been reporting on economic affairs, I have heard tales of ways in which countries – and their citizens – are the pawns of the great international institutions. It used to be the International Monetary Fund in Washington that pulled strings to choke the British economy; latterly, the European Common Market has had to take a lot of stick for 'wrongs' that are widely believed to be attributable to it. To some extent public reaction to the existence of such heavyweight and influential bodies truly reflects their power and the importance of their decisions. What they say certainly does matter, though it matters less than the decisions of national government and its agents. In this sphere it is the decisions taken in Whitehall or Washington, Paris or Bonn, that colour the lives of British or American people, the French or the Germans.

When it comes to making sense of the economy, the big decisions of the latter group claim the largest share of our attention. Small wonder people pay more heed to gossip about what the Chancellor of the Exchequer will do next than to the latest theory of a statistical professor or a stockbroker in the gold market: after all, the Chancellor has the power. (I well remember an occasion when a Chancellor of the Exchequer found himself, incongruously, at an international conference in a notorious gambling hotel. The one – unfulfilled – wish of the journalists was to secure a picture of the Chancellor playing one of the hundreds of fruit machines which crowded the place over the caption: 'Has he pulled the right lever?')

It comes down to this: governments and international institutions have the widest powers to affect the economic climate. The corporate decisions of the managers of the great multinationals and semi-state bodies profoundly affect employment, and prices, and services; and the personal decisions of the consumers, whatever pressures are laid on them by the other two, have the final say in the progress or otherwise of the economy.

And all of these decisions are based on information about the present state of affairs. At the beginning of a book which is intended to help, it is sad to have to say that no one ever really knows what the whole 'state of affairs' is, simply because there are so many conflicting factors bearing on the situation at any given moment that economic omniscience is impossible.

Nonetheless, the chapters which follow will attempt to chart the sources available, the ways of finding out about the trends, facts indeed fancies that form an important part of the economic climate, so that *Making Sense of the Economy* will be accessible, if not to that large group I mentioned earlier, whose minds switch off at the very word, at least to those companions who have got this far down the route without already wishing to write me long letters proving how wrong I am and sending me a panacea for all our ills.

# PART I

# Government Decisions

# 1
# The Budget Judgement

In the spring of 1981 there was the hell of a row. Senior Ministers in the Government, some of them in the Cabinet, were enraged that they had not been consulted about, let alone informed of, the changes in taxes and spending plans which went in to making up the 1981 Budget. Their rage spilt over into the following weeks, and when the measures which were to implement the Budget were presented in Parliament, the Tory 'rebels' caused at least one tax (the increase in diesel fuel duties) to be halved.

The row of 1981 was interesting because it concerned members of the Government party. It is to be expected that the Opposition will protest at every change in spending or taxation that the other side introduces (even if it would have done precisely the same things in office). On this occasion, however, there was a split in Conservative ranks, and the group of MPs and Ministers who disagreed with the Prime Minister, Mrs Thatcher, were described as 'wets'. Although their complaint was about the kind of policy which Mrs Thatcher and her Chancellor of the Exchequer, Sir Geoffrey Howe, intended to pursue – the 'wets' believed that it would lead to unpopularly high levels of unemployment – the focus of the row was that they were not told what would be in the Budget, nor indeed consulted in Cabinet until the day before the Budget speech and long after the government printing presses had started running off circulars to traders and wholesalers detailing the new rate of excise duty and the like.

The reason why they were so cross is that the Budget is important. It is almost always the most important economic event in the calendar for every household, every businessman and every politician in the country. (I say 'almost always' because there can be other, even more important decisions, like the devaluation of the pound in 1967 or entry into the European Economic Community (EEC), which have much greater consequences than an annual Budget, but they are rare.)

Faced with this extremely important and contentious issue, known in the jargon of government departments and economic discussion as the 'Budget judgement', how do the Chancellor of the Exchequer and his advisers know what to do? How, indeed!

The first guidelines in forming the Budget judgement come to the Chancellor and his fellow Ministers from exactly the same sources as would be consulted by any family conclave about making ends meet or any company meeting on financing the business. They are the accounts of how much is in hand by way of income, how much is likely to be spent in the coming year and, if there is to be a gap between the two, how much can reasonably be borrowed to bridge it.

This is the book-keeping aspect of government Budgets, and the information which comes into the great office of the Treasury, at the bottom of Whitehall, half-way between No. 10 Downing Street and Big Ben, is very reliable. From all the Departments of State come the estimates of their spending plans, and from the Inland Revenue service and the Customs and Excise come the estimates of tax revenues.

Very often in Parliament, in newspapers and elsewhere much is made of the difference between the published estimates of revenue and of expenditure in the Budget and what actually happens later, called the 'out-turn'. But it is comparatively rarely that these errors, which provide such ammunition for criticism, amount to more than a few percentage points. All the same, while they are small in percentage terms, they may have much larger implications. If total expenditure running at about £125,000 million a year is under-estimated by, say, 1.5 per cent and expected revenues are over-estimated by a similar error at, say, £118,000 millions for that year, the gap between the two would widen from the planned £7,000 million to over £10,500 million in the final event. The importance of such a change – of more than 35 per cent in the gap between income and spending – lies in the implications for public borrowing and interest rates discussed below.

But the Chancellor of the Exchequer and his advisers can be reasonably confident that the figures for spending by government departments (especially since the introduction of cash limits in the late 1970s) will be reasonably accurate, and figures for taxation income will also give them a starting-point.

They will also be told by their advisers in the City of London, consisting of the Bank of England and the Government Broker, what they will probably be able to borrow to meet the gap between revenue and expenditure and what is likely to happen to the rate of interest on borrowing which will flow from any level of government need for money, a larger amount of government borrowing leading to a higher rate of interest and vice versa. At this point in preparing his plans for a Budget the Chancellor and his team are moving away from the purely book-keeping aspect of counting up the incomings and outgoings and into the much less precise area of economic and financial policy.

In the minds of the Whitehall team working on the Budget will always be the question – which comes up again and again in the context of economic management and decisions – of the effect of their actions on confidence and the markets. There are many different ways in which the decisions taken at Budget time can affect the markets because there are many markets.

In the City of London alone there are markets for stocks and shares, for money itself (for raising mortgages, or borrowing among the banks) and for foreign currency, where dealers buy and sell pounds, dollars and so on. All the traders in all these different markets have different interests on Budget Day. What's 'good for the pound' may be bad for industry; but an opposite influence, which depresses confidence in the pound, may work to the benefit of consumers and therefore of industry. This is the beginning of the emergence of the problem which will run through many of the pages that follow – that making sense of the economy is as often a matter of judgement as it is a simple counting up of figures.

The two markets whose confidence can be affected by economic policy decisions, and especially by the Budget, are the markets for money at home and abroad. At its simplest, the foreign exchange market, where traders deal in the currencies of different countries, will react differently from the domestic money market (and the stock market), where the reactions to economic news are more parochial.

In the foreign exchange markets there is the additional complication that traders can hedge their bets by buying and selling in the 'forward' market, as we shall see in detail later on. This means that they take a view about what may happen in a few months' time and if (for instance) they expect the pound to fall in value, sell pounds *now* which may be bought back later more cheaply. Much of this dealing is done by traders who actually need the money for foreign business. Some is done by those who want to make money out of the market, the 'speculators', who are often attacked by politicians for upsetting the apple cart, from the 'Gnomes of Zurich' who were criticized by Lord George-Brown (then plain Mr) in the 1960s to the dealers who 'should have known better', in the words of Mrs Thatcher, commenting on a run on the pound in the winter of 1982–3.

Then, of course, there is institutional pressure from abroad. Britain is a member of the International Monetary Fund (IMF), which oversees and governs the world's international payments outside the Soviet bloc. There have been many occasions when British financial and Budget policy has been influenced by the IMF, the most striking recent case being the Budget of 1968, which followed the devaluation of the previous November and in which the thinking of the international economists at the IMF headquarters in Washington played a large part. On that occasion what was needed, according to the judgement of the IMF, was a tough Budget, with strict monetary controls on credit, in order to slow down the domestic economy and to allow industry to take advantage of the devalued pound to sell successfully abroad and deliver Britain from the crisis which had caused the devaluation in the first place.

Such dramatic interventions from Washington are rare, but the Chancellor of the Exchequer is aware that it is not just the confidence of individuals abroad that he is aiming to sustain but also that of the IMF and other important bodies to which Britain belongs, like the EEC and the Organization for Economic Co-operation and Development (OECD), whose role and importance is discussed in chapter 13, on international trade.

On all these the impact of the Chancellor's decisions will have different effects. For instance, a Budget proposal for higher interest rates is likely to suggest to foreign holders of pounds sterling, who have the freedom to switch their bank accounts or investments into other currencies, that the pound is worth holding on to, and it may even make the pound attractive to those who have been holding other currencies. They will see evidence that the Government wishes to strengthen the international value of the pound, and this perception will become self-fulfilling, as they decide to buy more pounds in exchange for their other national currencies.

But precisely the same measure may have the opposite effect on domestic confidence. Higher interest rates upset industrialists who have to pay for their new investment in equipment, factories, even advertising campaigns; and at the humbler scale of the consumer, higher charges for borrowing money may put off the buyer, leading to a slow-down in business and commerce, which can, if over-done, turn into a full-blown recession.

At the other end of a crudely conceived see-saw, lower interest rates announced in a Budget may engender confidence at home and doubts abroad. As Treasury officials are aware, there can be no certainty about the impact on confidence of any particular package of measures, but they are very conscious of the danger of going too far in one direction or another. The consequence is that as they draw up plans for the most momentous policy decision of the year, in the background there will be sensitivity towards what, simply put, they can 'get away with'.

Even with such limits to action, the Budget judgement nevertheless is not based entirely on cautious steering. Once the broad state of book-keeping is clear, the object of Budget strategy will be to improve the economic climate and to change the course of events in the shorter or longer term.

The influences which are brought to bear on the Budget judgement are as much political as economic. After gaining office at an election, the party in power will wish to influence society and its course by the Budget, as by other legislation, whether in the fields of education, immigration, criminal justice or equal opportunities.

In broad terms, the Budget judgement can affect the electorate in two ways: it can attempt to change the general level of economic activity by 'giving a boost' or by 'putting on the brakes' (to use the colloquialisms common in the papers the day after Budget Day), and it can redistribute wealth within the population by 'squeezing the rich' or by 'soaking the poor' (once more, according to headline taste the day after). The combination of objectives – trying to steer the whole economy and trying, within the whole, to achieve social change agreeable to the electorate and to the party in power – results in a complex set of pressures in the run up to Budget Day. When he stands up before the House of Commons the Chancellor of the Exchequer wishes to propose a plan which will please both his own party and the electorate at large, will not frighten the horses (in this case, the City, foreigners and businessmen) and will be within those housekeeping means of income and borrowing which his advisers allow.

There are opportunities for sensational reform. James Callaghan's Budgets of the mid-1960s, introducing Corporation Tax and the short-lived but provocative Selective Employment Tax, were such, when the Government chose to try to influence not only the short term by the balancing of the Budget but also the future through changes in the structure of taxation.

## Table 1   The Budget judgement

**1. Housekeeping: the opening position**
Next year's

| | |
|---|---|
| Revenue | £110,000 million |
| Spending | £115,000 million |
| Gap | £5,000 million |

**2. Economic position**
Unemployment rising
Production falling
Inflation falling
Interest rates down

Need for expansion of, say, £2,500 million

**3. Policy objectives**
To encourage incentive
To switch tax from income to spending
To reduce unemployment by direct spending

*The budget decisions*

| | |
|---|---|
| Cut income tax | −£2,000 million |
| Increase petrol, drink, tobacco duties | +£500 million |
| Increase public spending | −£1,000 million |

*Closing position*

| | |
|---|---|
| Revenue | £108,500 million |
| Expenditure | £116,000 million |
| Gap | £7,500 million |

To this imaginary Budget three considerations – (1) housekeeping, (2) the economic position and (3) policy objectives – have been simplified to show the sorts of decision which might confront the Chancellor of the Exchequer (and the Cabinet) in the early 1980s. The Budget decisions alter the opening position, which is the state of affairs that would persist if nothing at all were done on Budget Day. The economic position prompts the Chancellor to assume a Budget deficit of £7,500 million rather than £5,000 million, which would be the deficit if policies remained unchanged. The increase of £2,500 million in the gap between revenue and expenditure represents the amount of stimulus to the economy offered by this Budget, which will have to be weighed against its possible effects on confidence, interest rates and many other factors.

The Selective Employment Tax (SET) of 1966, for instance, was proclaimed as a deliberate attempt to shift the emphasis of economic activity into manufacturing industry – and consequently away from 'services'. The means to this end was a tax on all employees that was paid by their employers, but the tax was repaid to those who qualified for rebate as manufacturers. Like all new taxes, it was unpopular, the main charges against it being that it would push up prices and was complicated to run. Shortly before its repeal by the 1970 Conservative administration a study showed that the effect of SET may actually have been to *reduce* prices in the retail trade because it encouraged the development of self-service shops and supermarkets. It may stand as a good example of a tax which mixed the practical aim of raising money with the strategic one of engineering a shift in economic and business life. Many Budgets attempt such shifts, for political or idealistic reasons.

The first Budget of the 1979 Conservative Government was a combination of the ideal and the possible. Pledged at the election to cut personal taxes so as to increase initiative and individual satisfaction, the summer Budget did just that, with a sharp cut in income tax. But within the constraints of book-keeping the new Chancellor was unable to tilt the scales as much as he would have liked and had to raise a very large sum of money by virtually doubling the rate of Value Added Tax (VAT), thus spoiling the effect, for many households, of the incentives for a few.

These examples are just some from a long line of Budgets which have attempted to keep the economy on course without offending or enraging party or people. Another was the occasion when, in the spring of 1975, Denis Healey increased the rate of income tax.

During the preceding autumn wage claims from trade union negotiators, freed from the restraints of a formal incomes policy (ejected along with the Conservative administration the previous February), had been rising to considerable heights. In spite of a loosely formulated 'Social Contract', which suggested that trade unions bargainers should seek no more than would compensate their members for the rise in prices of the past year, the level of claims (and of settlements) was running very much higher than that. So towards the end of 1974 Denis Healey made a speech in which he declared that if by the time he had to make his Budget judgement the level of settlements was not a good deal lower than it looked like being, he would take back the excessive pay awards through income tax. It was no idle threat: he did it.

That was a particularly dramatic, and public, instance of a Chancellor's responding in a Budget to a changing economic scene. Usually the currents run more slowly, even for the whole year, in leading up to the March or April dénouement.

Work never ceases on the planning of the next Budget. Even as the Chancellor of the Exchequer sits down at the end of his 100-minute speech one Tuesday in March or April, someone, somewhere, is turning from the Radio 4 relay or the TV commentary on the speech to his or her files on the next stage of tax reform, or foreign aid, or industrial policy, which will later be fed into the pipeline for consideration next time round. Often these efforts are even mentioned in the speech itself; promises are made that next year this tax loophole or that new initiative will be dealt with.

Setting aside such long-running stories, however, the shape of Budget preparation goes something like this.

In early summer, when others' thoughts are turning to holidays and relaxation, the first stages of next spring's Budget are in preparation. Officials from the Treasury Department in Whitehall are, once more, sending their annual inquiries around to the other Departments which spend taxpayers' money. This is the work of the Public Expenditure Survey Committee (PESC), which simply asks the other Departments to declare their spending plans for the following year. It is the innocuous beginning of what is often a fierce battle.

When the figures have been received from all Departments, the Treasury makes its own estimates of the revenue to be expected from taxes, other sources such as the sale of public assets, EEC budget rebates and the like. By early autumn the Chancellor of the Exchequer is ready to go to Cabinet with the first stage of his plans for the following year. These are the totals of public spending which he is prepared to allow.

And this is where the battle hots up, for virtually all the other Ministers in the Cabinet run spending Departments and do not wish to see their programmes cut back, their spending reduced. Whatever the colour of the Cabinet, this battle between spending and saving Ministers is perpetual. It is sometimes complicated by other differences of opinion within the Cabinet. Thus in the autumn of 1981 the Cabinet was sharply split between those who wanted to see public spending (and hence public borrowing) sharply reduced, in line with the policy laid down by the Prime Minister, Mrs Thatcher, and her economic Ministers, and those who wanted to see a higher level of spending and borrowing for national economic reasons.

Whatever the arguments in Cabinet, by the end of the year the picture is beginning to form, and the Chancellor of the Exchequer has a clear idea how high the spending by Government and other public bodies is going to be in the coming year. He then has to decide on the other two components in the Budget judgement, taxation and borrowing.

It is at this stage, roughly between Christmas and Budget Day, that the advice and information that the Chancellor receives becomes crucial. By now he knows how much money he has to find – but there is more to making a success of the Budget than just getting the balance right. He and his advisers must first consider the existing state of the economy. They must answer these questions: is the economy running down, and is unemployment growing? Or are there signs of shortages ('over-heating', as its known) which could lead to higher pressures on wages and on prices, so that rising prices, and not rising unemployment, is the most important problem?

To make this judgement the Treasury needs information and opinion. There is no lack of either, but the sources available to the Chancellor can be roughly grouped as follows: in-house material, including all the figures compiled by the Central

Statistical Office or by government Departments such as the Departments of Employment, Trade and Industry; then the financial information from the Bank of England, which shows the pace of growth in money and credit; and finally the mass of information from outside the government's own machine.

In addition to compiling dry statistics, the Treasury has to assess the significance of this information and for this purpose uses the commonest tool of the practical economist, the model. A model is simply a set of mathematical equations designed to turn raw data into a picture of the economy on which to base the action to be taken in the Budget.

The next chapter discusses economic forecasts in greater detail and considers economic models. At this stage all that need be said is that the purpose of the Treasury model is to provide first for civil servants and then, through them, for the Ministers and the Chancellor of the Exchequer estimates of what will happen to the economy in the next year or so on the basis of various assumptions, including 'unchanged policies' – that is, what happens if the Chancellor does nothing – and, of course, the likely effects of the things he may want to do. The Treasury model, however sophisticated, nevertheless relies, as does the Chancellor, on the information available.

The quality of the advice and information that is put before the Chancellor is bound to be mixed. In general, the historical statistical data will be accurate – although revisions to provisional figures can often be large and make it unwise to base too much on early estimates – but the same cannot always be said of the interpretative advice which goes into making the Budget judgement, whether from inside or outside government.

In recent years, for instance, while the historical facts were known about the slowing down of economic activity in the early stages of the 1979 recession, the analysis and interpretation fell down badly because the final Budget judgement miscalculated the speed of decline in output and jobs. Thus in the event the Government needed to borrow far more than it had intended, as demands on its purse to pay unemployment benefit rose and receipts from income tax fell.

If that was an error inherent in the model of the economy, other forms of error, or dangerous ground, also appear in the run-up to decision day for the Chancellor. This is because so much of the advice he receives is partisan. From December onwards it is open season for organizations of all sorts to press upon No. 11 Downing Street their conflicting ideas and claims for the Budget. It is not just the obvious and vocal claims of such diverse interests as the Trades Union Congress (TUC) and the Confederation of British Industry (CBI) can be clearly seen to point in different directions, but also the less public though equally potent voices of the City of London, expressed through the Bank of England, or the building societies, representing owner-occupiers and home buyers.

While the Chancellor will have no difficulty in identifying the special interests of those who come to see him in the weeks before the Budget, his problem is how much weight to attach not only to what they say they want (which may be largely political and selfish in content) but also to what they tell him about the state of affairs in their industry. In the spring of 1982, for instance, the Chancellor accepted the CBI's plea of difficulty and reduced the surcharge that employers were paying on National Insurance – but only by half as much as they wanted. On a much smaller scale, he evidently heard and accepted the arguments of the Scotch whisky distillers, who had claimed that a large increase in tax on whisky would reduce the tax flow because consumption would fall dramatically. While it was evident to all that the distillers were trying to protect their own trade, the Chancellor decided that their deduction was also correct and increased the duty on whisky a good deal less than on other drinks. A great many other lobbyists were turned away empty-handed.

Faced with the mass of choices which go into every Budget, it is inevitable that some will turn out to be wrong. In 1979, for instance, high-ranking Ministers estimated that the summer increase in VAT to 15 per cent would 'work through' in a mere three months or so and would have no lasting effect on prices. With hindsight it is clear that the large rise in prices caused by the VAT increase remained a source of pressure for higher wage settlements for a full year, and that in turn made the Government's declared priority, to reduce the rate of price increases, far more difficult to achieve.

But there is a greater difficulty inherent in judging the effects of Budgets when they are being planned, which is when it matters. And this, the fundamental problem confronting anyone trying to make sense of the economy, whether the Chancellor or the private individual, is to guess correctly how people will react to the stimulus offered, or the restrictions imposed, by a Budget.

Let us take two parallel cases. In the early 1960s the American administrations of Presidents John Kennedy and Lyndon Johnson reduced taxes in successive Budgets to try to reduce unemployment in the United States. The effects were impressive – by 1965 unemployment had fallen fast, American output was rising rapidly and, significantly, prices had hardly gone up at all. The second case is that of the expansionary Budgets in Britain in the early 1970s, which, following the Kennedy–Johnson example, put money into the taxpayers' pockets and made credit amply available. But this time the consequence, though there was a fall in unemployment, was also an acceleration in wage and price levels, which eventually, through the imposition of a wages policy, led to the conflict with powerful trade union feelings, the miners' strike and the fall of the Government at the February 1974 general election.

Economists argue heatedly over why in one country at one time certain economic measures should produce results so dramatically different from those of the same measures at another time and in another country. Budgets will always be judged by their results, and these results are generally unpredictable, not least because any Budget is superimposed on an existing economy, which is not static but dynamic, for better or worse. It is therefore of the greatest importance that the Chancellor, along with everyone else in a successful economy, should have the keenest possible foresight when planning his next moves.

The instinct of the politician, the desire to win the next election by means of a Budget that will succeed, gives place, if error is to be avoided, to the voice – or, rather, the many voices, not all saying the same thing – of the forecasters.

# 2

# Forecasting the Economy

Forecasting is about the past. To illustrate this paradox outside the economic field: when the aircraft carrier HMS *Invincible* distinguished herself in the task force sent to relieve the Falkland Islands in the summer of 1982, she had already been promised for sale to the Australian Navy. There was a quick and understandable demand that she should be retained in the Royal Navy for future use – along with a number of other changes in naval policy that were hotly argued. In this case the trenchant *forecasts* of the ship's future usefulness were based on her very recent *past* performance in the South Seas.

Though infinitely more complicated than such immediate inferences, economic forecasting is based on the same essential premise: what has happened in the past is more likely than not to happen again. Out of this kernel of common sense a great industry of economic forecasting has grown up, not least within the Government itself and its many departments, local and central. Of what does it consist?

The art of forecasting is to choose those elements in the past which are most likely to repeat themselves and then to construct a set of equations of which the results (by reference to past experience) will suggest the shape of the future outcome.

Because we live in a moving picture – a 'dynamic economy', if you prefer – rather than in a still snapshot, it is quite easy to construct a simple forecast. Thus if the trend over a number of years has been for improved machinery and working methods ('technology') to increase the amount that any individual worker can produce in a factory, and that factor ('productivity') is rising faster than the total sales of the product, then it is not difficult to predict that employment in the factory will fall. But suppose that the salesmen from the factory offer the product at lower prices and are able, because of the higher productivity, to sell more of the goods than the number that simply reflects the increase in output per man, then the level of employment in that factory will surely rise.

In that example a proposition that seems obvious enough – that more modern techniques and machines will take jobs away from manual workers – collapses as a forecast when the next element, the consequence of lower prices, is also taken into account. It is the perpetual headache of the economic planner, whether the forecaster or the user of forecasts, that there are always a vast number of factors at play. Moreover, to some extent the forecasts vary because, with hindsight and close analysis, later critics can pinpoint things which forecasters have left entirely out of their calculations.

An illuminating example of this sort of miscalculation came twenty or thirty years ago, when the first computers were installed in the offices of stockbrokers in New York's Wall Street financial district. At first it was thought that one computer could do all the work of the clerks and secretaries who worked in the back offices of stockbroking firms, thus greatly reducing their need for space (since in any case some of the computers would be located in neighbouring New Jersey or Long Island and would be connected only by telephone wires to the scene of actual trading). In consequence, some of the shrewdest property firms forecast a big drop in the value of office space in downtown New York. However, when the computers arrived and were plugged in, the broking firms found that they could do far more than just the back-office book-keeping with them; the new machines, if properly fed with information, could analyse market trends, produce vast amounts of information, even attempt to pick winners on the Stock Exchange for the clients of the stockbroking houses. The result was an enormous expansion of staff needed to feed the computers with information – and in next to no time Wall Street property values were shooting up again.

No doubt a forecast could have been put together which would have spotted the extra work, and the extra saleable products of that work, which the computer would bring to the financial district of New York. If it had been, it would have needed to be an *imaginative* forecast. By that I mean a forecast which includes unknown elements and is not entirely reliant on looking at past trends and carrying those forward into the future. In the long run, the performance of forecasters will depend largely on how imaginative, and how well calculated, are their models.

In general, economic forecasts tend to be right, in spite of the popular conception that they, like the weather men, always get it wrong. The accuracy of forecasting is a consequence of the fact that forecasts are constructed around trends, not immediate results, as with horse race betting. (In this sense, economic forecasters enjoy an immunity not afforded to the weather men, who can equally be right in general, but if they are wrong about today, the picnic is ruined!)

The producers of forecasts have a lot to contend with, and they are by no means all doing the same things. In general, forecasts can be divided into three kinds. There are those which attempt to chart the future course of a process which is already taking place, such as changes in wages or prices (below I will give an example, albeit simple, of the way in which that sort of forecasting works). Then there is a rather different form of forecasting, the kind that is attempted when what is about to happen is new. Such forecasting includes, for instance, predictions about whether the exchange rate for the pound, or any other currency, will in future go up or down. Here the forecaster has plenty of data about the past but is faced with very great uncertainty about the future because he may not be discussing a 'trend' in which information about past changes actually affects future predictive results. Finally, there is forecasting in which nothing is known about either the future or the past: predicting the sale of a new product, for instance. As I write, breakfast television in Britain is in this category (though this is not quite a pure example: there has been breakfast TV in the USA for thirty years), and the skills needed to predict what market share it may get – indeed, may have already got by the time you are reading this – are very different from those required by the other main types of prophecy.

Economic forecasters all work from the same data, consisting of the records of the past. The variations between their predictions depend almost entirely on the weight that they afford to the different factors at work.

An economic forecast may be exceptionally simple, using only one set of figures, as, for example, predictions I have myself made about the future course of price inflation, which have on occasion turned out to be highly accurate and have given my colleagues occasion to ask, 'Who leaked the figures?' This simplest of forecasts works as follows. We have figures for every rise in the Retail Price Index (RPI) for the past twelve months; the commonly quoted one is the Annual Rate, that is, the amount by which the RPI is now higher than it was a year ago, expressed as a percentage. In early 1982 that figure was about 12 per cent.

I was credited with almost magical powers when I predicted at that time that the rate would soon drop to single figures. But the prediction was as safe as houses once the method was disclosed.

I knew from the past figures that in the three months March–May of 1981 the index had shot up by more than 5 per cent, almost entirely because of taxes sharply increased by the Budget, higher council house rents, higher rates and other charges. Once I knew – and this was public knowledge – what was in the March 1982 Budget (much smaller tax increases) and that rents, rates and so on were going to be increased by far less than they had been the year before, it was simplicity itself to see that in the annual comparison on which eyes are fixed, three months in which prices had risen by over 5 per cent were to be replaced by three months in which the rise was less than 3 per cent. And that was all it took to bring the inflation rate down to 9.5 per cent.

At the other end of the spectrum from that very simple piece of economic prediction is the vastly complicated 'macro-economic' model. There are scores of competing models, and, as I have mentioned, their predictions vary according to what is assumed at the starting-point, what, so to speak, is put into the mixture.

Without attempting to be comprehensive – there are literally thousands of variables in the more sophisticated models – these are some of the variables which occur in all such schemes:

> the exchange rate for the national currency against other currencies
> the value of imports, and exports
> the value of industrial production
> short- and long-term money interest rates
> employment and unemployment figures
> rates of pay
> productivity (that is, output per man)
> the value of consumers' spending
> the value of personal incomes
> the value of savings (which is personal disposable income *less* personal consumption, above)
> the value of total output in the economy
> the value of total spending in the economy
> the value of total investment in the economy
> housing construction
> retail sales
> etc., etc.*

Imagine that a forecast of the future course of any of these variables will depend, to some extent, on changes in some or all

---

* Many of these variables are going to come up again as we go along, in the chapters on output (3), inflation (5), employment and trade (10) and so on. Most of them are also listed in the list of sources on page 202, where chapter references to their main treatment can be found. At this point the important thing to grasp is that although they may seem separate, nearly all are directly or indirectly linked to the others.

of the others. The trick in good forecasting is to know how a change in one will produce a change in others or a chain reaction affecting all of them. Much of the forecaster's knowledge of these relations is based on the examples of the past: a good deal more is based on the theories of economists who say, for instance, that it is axiomatic that if the price of a particular commodity is reduced, more people with buy it. (This, though a prime tenet of economics, doesn't always happen in the real world!)

Because much of the shape of a forecasting model is based on the economic theories of the person who has constructed it, there is wide scope for different emphases within it. Thus a monetarist approach to forecasting will mean that the model will be heavily influenced by changes in the supply of money, however measured (see below, chapter 4, for details of such measurements and their importance). On the other hand, a fundamentalist economist (one who considers the volume of physical activity and financial trading, rather than the theory) may put more weight on such factors as output and employment, relegating changes in the supply of money to the status of a consequence, not a cause, of real change.

Given the broad spectrum of economic opinion, there can be very wide ranges of emphases in models, as I have pointed out. There are also, of course, many different end uses. Before surveying a handful of the best-known – and most seriously considered – of economic forecasts, it may be worth indicating that it is not only the creative imagination of the author of the economic model which may make it more or less successful, as suggested above, there are also fundamental differences of approach.

For example, there is the puzzle already referred to of how much a change in the measured supply of money in the economy (known to the forecasters and bureaucrats as 'monetary aggregates') affects the future. Here the differences of treatment can be quite fundamental: will the movements in money affect wages, or prices, or real output? This is a highly complex field, within which economists differ sharply, not usually about the relationships in *time* between, say, a rise in the supply of money and a rise in either production or prices, but about the relationships of *cause*. Some of these problems will be discussed later on, in chapter 4 and elsewhere, but for the moment back to the forecasters.

In chapter 1 I mentioned the Treasury model used by government to make its predictions about the future course of events. Here the purpose is clear: to tell the Chancellor of the Exchequer and his Ministers what will happen to employment, to prices, to Britain's foreign payments prospects if he does nothing or if he does any of the many things open to him in the way of policy changes. He wants the clearest possible picture, and he wants reliable predictions of a variety of outcomes based on different tax rates, interest rates and so on – a bird's-eye view of the economy in its entirety.

Other forecasts are more modest, focusing, say, on the prospects for a single industry or concerning themselves with financial predictions, such as how the stock market will perform, how interest rates or foreign currency exchange rates will move.

Forecasts can be categorized not only by subject matter (what they attempt to predict) but also by source. There are, obviously, both commercial and academic forecasts, private and public, official and freelance.

At the time of writing, there are half a dozen or so 'heavy' forecasts for the British economy, apart from the Treasury forecasts which are doled out so discreetly that they hardly count. Close to the official model, in that the arithmetical bases are much the same, is the quarterly *National Institute Economic Review*. In the past the National Institute of Economic and Social Research has earned a good name for thoroughness and accuracy and for the distinctive tone of the recommendations for public policy with which it garnishes the quarterly review. Thus it has frequently advocated 'incomes policies', and argued for 'expansionary' economic policies in time of high unemployment. If a judgement is to be made, this kind of advocacy places the Institute at the centre, or perhaps slightly to the left of centre, of the spectrum of economic argument. (It is by no means way-out: for many years the Bank of England's *Quarterly Bulletin* took a more favourable view of incomes policies than did the official Whitehall line, giving such policies the solid backing of the country's premier financial institution!)

Further to the 'left', is the Cambridge University Department of Applied Economics' team of forecasters. In recent years the Cambridge economists have consistently predicted worsening conditions in the British economy, and they have often been roundly confirmed in their forecasts which have predicted higher unemployment and deeper slump than made by more orthodox or cautious forecasters. In their prescriptions too the Cambridge team are often more radical than the mainstream; for instance, they are advocating import controls to protect jobs in Britain at a time when the 'right' are urging the freest of free trade to keep economies going. In this sense Cambridge and the National Institute suggest more intervention by the state to try to set things right, whether with controls on wages or prices or with restrictions on imports.

The London Business School, another of the heavyweights in the forecasting business, received an accolade when Dr Terry Burns, one of the senior economists practising there was appointed chief economic adviser at the Treasury under the Prime Ministership of Mrs Thatcher, leaving his colleagues, led by Dr Alan Budd, to carry the torch of monetarism in forecasting. It would be quite unfair to say that its forecasts were ever seriously tilted by the 'right-ish' influence of monetarism and market forces, though in the early 1980s they had a very different flavour from the Cambridge or National Institute surveys. In general supportive of the kind of economic policy being carried through by Mrs Thatcher, the London Business School's reviews became progressively more cautious about the economic outlook as the recession deepened.

These are only three of the forecasts produced quarterly, half-yearly or occasionally by many institutions. I referred to the Bank of England's *Quarterly Bulletin*; but while the Bank's economic department undoubtedly has strong views about the future course of events and, as I have suggested, often tussles with the Treasury when not in agreement with the political end of the road from the City of London to the Palace of Westminster, it does not regularly publish detailed forecasts. The reader of the *Bulletin* has to glean for himself, from remarks in the text, what the Bank thinks is going to happen next.

If the Bank of England goes on record once every three months, a full disclosure of the Treasury's thinking is far harder to come by – or, paradoxically, far easier. The most complete outline of the Government's own forecast of the state of the economy comes, naturally enough, with the Budget. It takes the form of the *Financial Statement and Budget Report* (FSBR), and it attempts to forecast the broad outlines of the economy over the months ahead. But even then, when the Government's mind is supposed to be open to inspection, there are obscurities.

The Budget Speech and the accompanying paperwork, including the FSBR, are usually cautious, for instance, about predictions concerning the future course of that most sensitive of issues, unemployment. Indeed, the whole of Budget Day can pass without any precise figure being set for what the Government expects to happen to unemployment. Apart from general remarks, the closest guide to what the official view is has to be sought in the annual White Paper on public expenditure, published a few weeks ahead of the Budget, which includes an 'assumption' about unemployment in the coming year – an assumption which is needed in order to work out how much unemployment pay will have to be found.

The Government's reticence about its own view of the future – perhaps understandable in the light of the wide errors of forecasting which have been made in the past – has nonetheless provoked a strong reaction from Parliament. As a result, after a number of years of pressure from the House of Commons and, latterly, from a new committee set up to oversee the Treasury and the Civil Service, a formal statement is now made in late October or November, which not only announces a number of small adjustments to Government economic policies but also contains a brief forecast of Government expectations for the future, albeit pretty limited in detail.

On the other hand, it is not difficult to learn roughly what the Treasury forecast is showing from time to time if you're prepared to interpret it through the filter of the speeches of Treasury and other Ministers in the House of Commons or on their stumps around the country. These speeches often give a glimpse of the direction that Ministers believe events are taking, and that direction is itself, to a greater or lesser extent, informed by the Treasury forecasting machine. (There are occasional lapses. In 1982, when one Cabinet Minister produced a 'forecast' that the cost of the Falklands campaign might mean higher taxes – a view quite contrary to Treasury orthodoxy – I asked Treasury officials why. I was told that the Minister concerned had not, perhaps, consulted them first!)

But, subject to such pitfalls and always allowing for a range of opinion to be expressed simultaneously by members even of the same party, it is possible to acquire some feel for the official view of the state of future affairs from reports of Ministers' speeches in the newspapers and statements expressing satisfaction or concern on the occasion of the monthly announcement of some important indicator such as unemployment or retail prices.

There is no need for the amateur of economics to feel bound to heed the prophecies of the forecasters, and the next few chapters outline ways in which you can form a view of the economy by going direct to the publicly announced figures themselves and reading in them, as in tea leaves, which way the wind is blowing.

# 3

# Jobs and Production

Until the late 1970s unemployment in Britain was often perceived as a temporary, albeit worrying, addition to dole queues, a social evil which had been largely banished since the Second World War but which inevitably rose by a few hundred thousand during the 'stop' phases of 'stop-go' economic performance. But since the onset of the greatest post-1930s recession and the steady climb of those out of work to 3 million people, unemployment has been clearly seen as the other side of the coin of contraction in British industry. This trend, for instance, has seen the closure of innumerable factories, whole vast steelworks, textile mills and tyre plants and the vanishing of countless companies and firms from the industrial scene for ever.

Then there came together, in their concern for the future of Britain, voices as disparate as those of Mr Tony Benn and the leadership of the CBI. As Mr Benn put it, what we were seeing was the erosion of the 'industrial base' of the country: the CBI were equally clear in their representations to Government that the recession was dangerously increasing the number of bankruptcies and closures.

The activities thus threatened are, of course, at the very heart of a mature industrial economy like Britain. Whether regarded as providing the occupation and means of earning a livelihood of the labour force or as the sources of the goods and services produced and consumed in the country, employment and the production of goods and services (output) are the very key to prosperity, the factors which differentiate the 'rich' countries of the world from less developed rural or semi-rural economies.

Curiously, though close attention is paid to the unemployment figures by politicians and by commentators, the statistics that measure the positive side of the economy – the actual production of goods and services – attract much less public attention. This may be partly because a rise in the unemployment figures prompts calls for action by the Government and a fall in unemployment equally produces smug satisfaction on the part of the Government that it has achieved something, whereas a rise or fall in the country's industrial production, or Gross National Product (GNP), attracts to the central Government neither praise nor blame – except over the long term – because such changes are seen as the sum of thousands of small decisions taken by merchants, by firms, by individuals.

With the exception of such political radicals as Mr Benn, who believes that government can influence production directly, most people seem to suppose that overall prosperity is a fact of life and history but that when it comes to unemployment, something must be done. If something is to be done, decisions made, actions taken, then it is obviously vitally important to know where the economy stands at any given moment.

There are several broad measures of the country's output and performance, which is called the Gross Domestic Product (GDP). The two most regularly charted by the Government's Central Statistical Office are the 'output' and 'expenditure' measures. Simply put, the 'output' measure is a census of the production of all activities in the country. It includes industrial production and the measurable contribution to activity of things like transport, services, local and central government and the like. The 'expenditure' measure of GDP approaches the problem from the opposite end, measuring as far as possible all the spending in the country, whether on goods bought for consumption or for capital investment or on services and, of course, including the expenditure of government, central and local. In theory, since GDP is an attempt to chart all economic activity in the country, the 'output' measure and the 'expenditure' measure should add up, roughly, to the same amount.

There are differences, of course. The 'output' measure includes goods produced in the country but sold abroad, exports
which do not show up in the 'expenditure' side. But 'expenditure' includes spending on imports which do not feature in the
'output' measure. So one would expect the 'output' measure to
be larger than the 'expenditure' measure when the country as a
whole is in surplus and exporting more than it is importing.
And vice-versa.

There are many refinements of measures of GNP, or the
National Income, as it is sometimes called. Different organizations produce divergent estimates, and the official statistics are
subject to many revisions. They appear first as 'provisional'
figures , then as 'revised' and eventually in their 'final' form
being recorded as historical data in the columns of last year's
statistics or even those of the year before.

One important concept to grasp when looking at these
figures is the difference between 'money GNP' and 'real GNP'.
Simply put, the census or monitoring of output done quarterly
– or, in some cases, monthly – is measured in current prices.
The question put is: 'What is the value of your output or
expenditure?' The answers, when all the figures are added up,
give the current value of GNP. But, as we all know, the value
of money is constantly changing; the change is downwards
nowadays, but there were times (for instance, in the pre-war
Depression) when prices fell and the value of money rose.

So economists have devised a way round the fluctuating
value of money when they want to chart things like GNP,
personal income or the like. They fix on a year in the past and
follow closely changes in prices for all goods and services since
that year. Then, when each new figure from GNP is produced,
they revalue it by the amount of the price change. It is an
artificial business, of course, producing in inflationary times a
much smaller 'real GNP' than the actual business activity
which has taken place in the period measured. But 'real GNP'
is a vital tool for decision-taking and for anyone charting the
progress or otherwise of the economy. This is because although 'money GNP' will include changes in prices, it will not

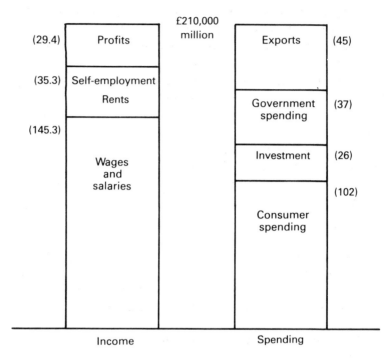

National income accounts are kept to show where the money comes from (seen here on the right as spending) and where it goes to (shown on the left as income). Exports are included in spending because foreigners buy part of what is produced in the United Kingdom. The total of all that spending equals total income, which goes to those who receive it in the form of wages, rent, self-employed income or profits. The figure shows that total income, even less profits, is a great deal larger a share of national income than is consumer spending. Part of that difference is represented by taxation, which appears here as part of total Government spending.

Source: Author's estimates based on official figures in Central Statistical Office, *Economic Trends*, London, HMSO, various issues.

Figure 1   National income and expenditure, 1981 (£000 million)

tell planners, whether in government or in public or private companies, what is actually happening in the real world. (Of course, one of the things that is happening in the real world is that prices and wages are going up or down – movements discussed in chapter 5 – but the real issue is how much of this is going on, not at what price.)

For example, spending on education may rise dramatically over a number of years. Much may be made of this in public debate. Turning 'money' spending on education into 'real' spending may, when changes in such things as the price of school heating and the level of wages are taken out of the figures, reveal a drop in 'real' spending. This calculation in turn can be further refined by dividing each year's figure by the number of children receiving education to arrive at 'per capita' spending on education.

The same is true of GNP. 'Money GNP' tells the observer little; it represents the raw material gathered at the factory, the school, the government Department. 'Real GNP', and more especially the changes in 'real GNP' from year to year, tell one a great deal – in a nutshell, whether the country is, economically speaking, growing, or stagnating, or in decline. Finally, 'per capita GNP', which allows also for changes in population, tells one whether the country is getting richer or poorer.

Those are the broad-brush measures of the output of the economy, vital for economists, historians, civil servants and, most of all, for politicians whose success or failure may, in the end, depend on how 'per capita GNP' is moving. But for others there are less sweeping, more focused measures of economic activity and output.

Included in the GNP figures is 'industrial production', which is calculated monthly by the Central Statistical Office as an index. It is by no means a perfect measure of what is going on, but it does give a more frequent, if rough-and-ready, guide to the state of affairs than do the quarterly GNP figures. One snag about the index of industrial production is that it is produced a couple of months after the event; revisions to the provisional figures can often be as large as, or larger than, the movements of the index itself from month to month, so that a small rise or fall may later be revised to show an opposite result.

All the same, the general movements in the index do give a fairly accurate picture of what is going on in industry. The index also points up where the action is. Thus the total index includes the mining, quarrying and North Sea oil industries, as well as manufacturing production. But the various components in the index are also charted separately, so that at a time of rising output it is possible to tell whether it is, for instance, the motor industry, or steel-making that is prospering.

A much more detailed analysis of what is going on in industry, which also has the merit of some elements of forecasting, is the CBI's quarterly *Industrial Trends Survey*. Once every three months about two thousand companies are asked a handful of questions about their immediate prospects and past performance. The central question is perhaps the least informative. It asks: 'Are you more confident of prospects now than four months ago?', and it gives the respondents the choice of answering 'more', 'less' or 'the same'. When all the answers are in, the CBI calculates a 'balance' of optimism or pessimism among the respondents by subtracting the more confident from the less or vice versa. Such changes in sentiment provide at best a crude guide to industrial climate, but there is much more than that to the *Industrial Trends Survey*. Each firm is asked whether it is booking more or fewer orders; whether it expects to be investing more or less money in equipment and buildings over the next year than the last; what factors (for example, lack of orders, lack of equipment) are inhibiting its sales; and whether it is making full use of its capacity. The answers to these detailed questions give a very accurate picture of what is going on in the many groups of industries into which the survey is broken down. It also provides a guide to export prospects and provides early warning of changes in inflation by asking firms whether they expect to be charging higher prices in the future.

Altogether, the *Industrial Trends Survey* is a useful pulse and has set a good track record for forecasting industrial investment, for instance, as the responses to the investment intentions question covering the year ahead are a very good guide to what will actually happen – and, indeed, to what has happened when a year or so later, the actual figures for factory building, machinery replacement and the like are duly published by the Department of Industry.

Another key measure of industrial health, which is charted by both government and the CBI, is the movement in stocks held by industry. This has become particularly significant in the 1980s.

All industrial concerns naturally hold stocks of goods and of materials in hand. The materials and components used for manufacture are essential. So too is a reasonable supply of finished goods, ready to be supplied to customers. However, both materials and finished goods are expensive to hold, since they have been paid for but are not yet earning a return. In good times firms and businesses tend to allow stocks to rise, anticipating higher sales; they are able to meet the cost of carrying stocks out of current business. On the other hand, signs in the *Industrial Trends Survey* or in the official quarterly government figures that the level of stocks held is stagnant or falling often accompany the onset of 'bad' times. In 1980 and 1981 stocks were cut back very sharply indeed. That part of the recession, during which 1.5 million people lost their jobs, many in industry, was described as a 'stock recession', or 'destocking'. The point was that in spite of rising incomes in the hands of consumers and an absolutely steady sale of goods in the retail trade, so that in terms of prosperity there seemed to be almost no down-turn at all, manufacturing industry was suffering an abrupt and dramatic reverse. The cause seems to have been largely the official policy of very high interest rates for money. In consequence, every business, from primary manu-facturer to distributor, wholesaler and retail shop, wanted to reduce its stocks, in order to move these expensive items on to someone else's shelves, where someone else would be paying the interest.

The success of stockholders of all sorts in getting rid of

goods was readily apparent. Shops ran sales at great length; prices for many goods, especially clothing and household items, were held down fiercely to tempt buyers and for those commodities did not rise at all throughout 1981. At the same time, everyone tried to cut down on their orders, and for well over a year the main sufferers from this squeeze were the original suppliers, the manufacturers. Whether it was raw steel, components or the whole finished good, demand from industry was hard-hit, and there followed the closures, bankruptcies and losses already noted. And, apart from a parallel set-back in the housing and construction market, the sole cause of the crisis was 'destocking'.

Finally, in the *Industrial Trends Survey*, there is the crucial question which links the two sides of the industrial coin. Each enterprise is asked: 'Do you expect to increase or decrease your labour force in the next four months?' Here is the tip of the iceberg in recording perhaps the most politically sensitive of all the economic indicators, unemployment. When the intentions of CBI members and of the rest of the economic scene are translated into fact the results are clear for all to see and to chart.

The Department of Employment produces the monthly count of the unemployed on the basis of returns from employment exchanges all over the country. It is more than just a head count, for the statisticians divide the unemployed into groups. There are the adult wholly unemployed; there are the temporarily stopped; there are the school leavers. The figures are also divided into those who have been out of work for longer or shorter periods. Observers pay particular attention to the number of people who have been out of work for more than a year, for instance; when that figure rises the situation is clearly more than usually grave. And, of course, the figures are broken down by region, employment black spots spreading like ink on blotting paper as the recession deepens.

For example, in good times the West Midlands is one of the few areas of Britain which actually makes ends meet, where unemployment is so low and wages so relatively high, that the product from taxes and rates and so on amounts to more than is used up locally in social services, education, housing, hospitals and the like. Consequently, there is a surplus of revenue which can go towards meeting the yawning deficits of other areas like Scotland, Northern Ireland or the north-east. (South-east England, the Aberdeen oil belt, Bristol and Yorkshire are the only other regions regularly in 'surplus'; all the rest need support from outside, or contribute to the general national shortfall.) However, in the 1980 recession the change in unemployment was nowhere more dramatic than in the West Midlands. In other regions chronic unemployment worsened, depression intensified: in the West Midlands the change was catastrophic, as the main employer on which so much depended, the motor industry, slumped.

There is much argument over the validity of the unemployment figures. People claim, sometimes with vested interests in mind, that they under- or overstate true unemployment. For example, some say that a number of the out-of-work are not actively seeking work, are 'unemployable', layabouts, scroungers (or whatever epithet suits the speaker's temper). It is argued with equal force, on the other hand, that many are 'missed' by the employment count, such as married women who move in and out of the labour force rapidly and are not necessarily registered when not working, and there may be other hidden unemployment, which gives proponents of this view excuse for adding, say, another million to the official total.

In one way none of this matters. The figures are at least collected and published in a consistent way. What they tell us about the economy is the direction in which things are moving: it is therefore the changes in the unemployment figures that are significant. In social and political terms, of course, the absolute totals matter very much indeed. Policies are argued and elections fought, from the local council to the general election, on the issue of unemployment. For months in 1982 – and later – 'unemployment' consistently scored the highest number of points as a response to the question put by opinion pollsters:

'What is the most important problem of the day?' Curiously, the emergence of this major preoccupation did not coincide with a serious loss of popularity for the party of the Government which had held power during the sharpest rise in unemployment. Perhaps people did not blame the Government; perhaps their party preferences were formed by non-economic considerations like defence or law and order or for economic reasons which offset against the rise in unemployment improved industrial performance and better prospects for prices.

And unemployment is of course of overriding importance to the individual confronted with joblessness now or in the future. I will be considering the consequences of the recession for the individual in chapter 18, but let me return to the overall figures whose movements up or down are so informative to economists.

Along with the unemployment figures come also the figures for job vacancies. Although they are not always a reliable guide, the vacancies notified to labour exchanges do, again, reflect the underlying trends in the economy and can, for instance, hold out hope for better things when they rise or threaten worse times ahead when they decline.

One further thing needs to be said about following the unemployment figures. Like many another series used by economists, the figures are 'seasonally adjusted'. This means that as well as simply counting heads, the statisticians try to work out which changes in levels are simply associated with seasonal patterns of work. This they do by reference to past years, deducing from what has happened in the past the allowances which should be made for things like weather and holidays. 'Seasonal adjustment' sometimes provokes the complaint that the figures are in some way 'fudged' or more difficult to understand; and at some times of year (for instance, at the end of school terms) the gross figures for unemployment may move in a different direction from the adjusted figures. That may give rise to confusion for headline writers, so that one newspaper, used to dealing with the 'real' world, cites a rise in unemployment, while another, more sophisticated, points up the fall in the seasonally adjusted total.

Both sets of figures have their validity. The adjusted ones tell us more about what is happening and is likely to happen as the trend of employment shifts, while the unadjusted, crude figures tell us more about where special help may be needed and, indeed, about the cost, not seasonally adjusted, of paying people not to work. That toll, not the least of the costs of unemployment, which also include the personal and family costs and the national waste of potential, is one of the burdens which fall on government spending, and it is just one of the many factors which influence the financial and monetary policy of a government.

# 4

# The Business of Money

In 1977 the compilers of the Supplement (containing 'new' words) to the great *Oxford English Dictionary* had reached the letter M. As the editor, Dr Robert Burchfield, later recounted, they came as near as a toucher to leaving out 'monetarism'. Yet from that very year making sense of the economy, and especially of government policy, has been dominated by the theory and practice of monetarism. It was in 1977 and in the next year that the Chancellor of the Exchequer, Denis Healey, presented monetarist Budgets before seeing the job handed over by the general election in 1979 to his successor Sir Geoffrey Howe, and his boss, Margaret Thatcher.

*Pace* the Oxford Dictionary, monetarism has been with us for a long while and stems from what economists call the quantity theory of money. This rests on the hypothesis that money, like any other commodity, may rise or fall in value compared with other goods. From this starting-point it is evident that if there is a growth in the availability of money compared with other goods, the 'price' of money will fall and the prices of other goods will rise; thus what is now known as inflation takes place. (The word 'inflation' in this context refers to the inflation, as of a balloon, of the supply of money; but for economists so strong is the link between this phenomenon and the ensuing rise in the price of other goods that the word 'inflation' has become synonymous with the rise in prices itself.)

But to come back to monetarism. The bedrock of the argument is this equation: $MV = PT$, where $M$ = money, $V$ = velocity of circulation of money; $P$ = price and $T$ = transactions. Translated: money times velocity of circulation must be equal to price times the number of transactions. The terms of the equation are such that in dealing with a money economy (that is, excluding barter, etc.), it must be true. The question is whether it tells us anything.

Here is where the great arguments for and against monetarism begin. The monetarists hold that if there is a rise in $M$, there will inevitably be a rise in $P$, so that the two sides of the equation remain in balance. The mechanism for the rise they call inflation. In modern times the guru of monetarism is Professor Milton Friedman of the University of Chicago, who has argued long and strenuously that if governments succeed in limiting the rise in $M$ to the rise in $T$ on the other side of the equation (that is, the amount of economic activity taking place, determined by rising population, new inventions, technology and so on), there will be no room for any rise in $P$, and prices will be stable.

For many onlookers the notion of monetary policy is different from Professor Friedman's rather austere formulation. They believe that changing the money supply may be useful in controlling the economy itself, so that a change, deliberately engineered, in $M$ may directly affect $T$: thus an increase in hire purchase credit may increase the sales of motor cars or fridges.

At the other end of the spectrum of theory are those who do not believe that the supply of money is the determining factor: they think: that what matters is what people go out and do. The money – only, after all, a means of exchange – will be provided to facilitate whatever level of growth the economy can achieve. These observers can also be accommodated by $MV = PT$. Their interest begins with $T$. If the economic climate is such that $T$ (the output of the economy in real terms, described in chapter 2) rises, then without there being any need for $P$ (prices) to go up $MV$ can also rise. And, they say, the rises or falls on the left of the equation need not all be in $M$; some may be in $V$, the velocity of circulation. In short, they deny the absolute importance of changes in money supply in influencing prices. And they can point to periods when, in spite of successful efforts to curb the supply of money, prices have gone on rising and times when prices have fallen although the money supply has been restricted. (There was the occasion in the early 1980s when the rate of price increase fell rapidly; that is, $P$ was rising more slowly. At the same time $T$ was actually falling – the beginning of the recession described in the last chapter. From this it might be assumed that M would also be in decline, or steady. Not a bit of it: $M$ was rising fast. The anti-monetarists claimed that $V$, the velocity of circulation, was also falling, thus breaking the monetarists' strict link between the amount of money and prices.)

In all this a key part in the equation is played by $V$. At its simplest the velocity of circulation means the speed at which money changes hands, evidently faster at the races or at a dog track than in the Reading Room of the British Museum. In the economy as a whole changes in velocity may arise from various causes. One may be the pace of activity itself, so that in good times people may be doing more business and shifting money out of savings into spending. This tends to increase both $M$ and $V$ in the equation, but at different speeds. Then a rise in prices and wages also causes a rise in velocity, simply because the amount of money changing hands in a year is higher, so that, measured against the paper worth of wages or prices, the flow or velocity rises for no better reason than that the value of money has fallen and more has to be paid out for the same value. As surmised above, velocity can also fall, in essence when people are slowing down their pace of spending for one reason or another.

As I hope the foregoing has shown, the debates about monetarism can be complicated even when limited to discussing the simple quantity formula. What matters in everyday life is how these arguments affect policy and decision-taking and how one can hope to understand what is going on in what one might call the 'money economy'.

The first, most universal barometer is interest rates. (It is therefore a thumping inconvenience to economy-watchers that the old bank rate, set by the Bank of England and published in the serious press, has been abolished, but more of that anon.) For the casual observer the guiding rate is nowadays the clearing banks' base rate, the basis on which they calculate the rates charged to customers according to their standing: a large company may be able to borrow at '1 over base', you or I at 2 or 3 per cent more.

The importance of base rate and other money-market interest rates is not only that they are an indicator of what borrowing money will cost but also that they provide a clue to the way in which the economy is moving. Falling interest rates are in general seen as likely to promote more economic activity, even greater prosperity or, at worst, recovery from slump. Rising rates suggest, to use that favourite colloquialism again, a 'touch of the brakes', discouragement of higher spending or of investment.

While that proposition remains true as a rough and ready guide to sentiment and to what is likely to happen in future, there are complexities. Even though, as I have said, bank rate has been abolished and even the more pompously entitled 'minimum lending rate' of the Bank of England also publicly suppressed, this does not mean that the Bank and the Treasury do not try to influence interest rates from time to time.

In this endeavour the Bank of England has a number of weapons. The first is sheer influence itself. As a Deputy Governor of the Bank once told me in his splendid office, one advantage of its location at the heart of the City was that it was within five minutes' walking distance (from them to him) of the offices of the chairmen of the big four banks! Second, the Bank, like any other bank in the City, deals in the inter-bank market for money and, by announcing at what rate it will deal, can therefore influence extremely short-term interest rates. Then it has the arcane but vital tool, the sale each week of Treasury bills. These are promises to pay, issued by the Government and sold by the Bank of England, through a handful of specialized firms called discount houses, to the general banking system. 'T-bills', as they are known in the City vernacular, carry no interest rate but are sold to the discount market at, as the name implies, a discount below the face value at which they will be repaid. Maturing (that is, being repaid) at from seven to ninety-one days, the depth of the discount at which they are sold that week sets the rate of interest for the period ahead.

By whatever means, then, the Authorities (as for convenience one often describes the alliance of Bank and Treasury to avoid too precise an attribution of initiative between them) can set interest rates. They will normally influence them for the sort of simple motive given above, to quicken or restrain the economic pace in the country. But because there is a large *international* aspect to the money economy – because British residents are free to move their wealth abroad, foreigners to bring theirs to Britain and, even more important, because more than a quarter of everything purchased in Britain comes from abroad – the Authorities have to keep a constant eye on the rates of interest in other countries. Their decisions will thus be influenced by the overall world scene. Where should the pound sterling stand against the US dollar or the French franc?

The dilemma about the international value of the pound is simple. If the pound stands high by comparison with the currencies of the countries with whom Britain trades, imports from those countries will be cheaper, from exotic produce from bananas and tobacco (which we cannot grow here), to the goods like textiles and footwear which we can and do produce, but at prices higher than those of foreign competitors and, finally, to high-technology products in which Britain has done better at invention than at production.

In all these fields a 'strong' pound encourages British consumers to buy foreign goods and, when it comes to such essentials as oranges, tea and the nickel from which knives and forks are made (and none of these is indigenous to Britain), allows them to buy more cheaply than when the pound is 'weak'.

A 'weak' pound, however, while increasing the cost to the British user of foreign goods, whether manufacturer or final consumer, makes the output of British industry cheaper for foreign buyers than it would otherwise be. So, when British goods seem relatively cheap in the world market more may be bought, and British business may prosper.

The influence of interest rates on the international value of the currency is direct. Banks – and other bodies like local authorities and industries which borrow money through the City – compete not only with each other but also with the rest of the world. So if interest rates in London move upwards against rates in New York or Frankfurt, lenders of money may switch their funds to London. This in turn will lead to bidding for pounds in the foreign currency markets, as foreign lenders try to take advantage of the higher rates. Since currency markets are now uncontrolled, that will mean a rise in the relative price of pounds *vis-à-vis* the rest. Equally a fall in London interest rates will have the opposite effect. As we have seen, a fall in the international value of the pound tends to increase prices at home but adds to sales of British goods abroad; a higher rate caused by higher interest rates will have the opposite effect – cheaper imports but lower foreign sales. A fuller discussion of the importance of international trade and the value of the pound is to be found in chapter 13, but at this point suffice it to say that the choice between high rates of interest and a 'strong' pound or low ones and a 'weak' pound may be difficult to make.

In the early 1980s it was argued, for instance, that the pound stood unduly high because of high interest rates and foreign investors' knowledge of the vast reserves of North Sea oil. This meant that while the cost of living rose more slowly because foreign goods imported into Britain were cheaper, unemployment in Britain rose more sharply because sales of British goods, now more expensive, fell both at home and abroad. Conversely, it was argued that the 'high' pound bought everyone a slightly higher standard of living and that greater efficiency would overcome the barrier to foreign sales that had been raised. This particular argument is never resolved, as will become apparent in later chapters on inflation and foreign trading. But it is perhaps less important when it comes to setting interest rates than in the context of domestic household management.

The Conservative Government of 1970–4 abandoned some of the last remaining vestiges of post-war controls on money and banking. Under the banner of a new policy called 'competition and credit control' the old formal controls on lending by bankers to industry and individuals were wound up. Until then the Bank of England had been able to impose quantitative controls on bank lending: thus if one of the clearing banks had lent £x million pounds in one year, it might be told that it could lend no more than £x + 10 per cent the next year. Instead, the banks, under the sort of guidance referred to above, were now to influence the borrowing of their customers not according to the *fiat* of the Bank of England but according to the level of interest rate charged, and occasionally in response to a 'letter' from the Bank of England suggesting to the banking system that, for instance, loans to industry for new factories and equipment should take priority over private loans for domestic redecoration, colour TVs or Spanish holidays.

Even while this relaxation of controls was going on – and, as we shall see later, it opened the door to the infamous 'secondary banks', which attracted funds from short-term depositors at rates higher than those of the 'square' clearing banks and then invested the money in long-term and unsuccessful property ventures, only to have their customers bailed out by the stolid old 'squares' in the end – it was becoming apparent that the 'money economy' was heavily influenced by the Government's own behaviour. In brief, the perception was growing that government borrowing was a factor which had almost more influence on the 'money economy' – and, indeed, still does – than anything else.

The borrowing of government includes, of course, that of local authorities and (from central funds) of nationalized industries operating at a loss. From the fact that most such 'public' activities constituted a drain on the national income, and the related perception that the ordinary revenues from taxation, excise duties and the like were not enough to meet the needs of the public sector, arose the profound worry that the populace at large was not 'paying its way'. At its most acute, this economic worry is expressed in such terms as 'Can we afford a National Health Service for all?', and one of the most startling consequences of the perception that you cannot go on borrowing money for unprofitable enterprises for ever was the famous Dr Beeching's brief to render the recently nationalized railway network less costly to the Exchequer by cutting out unprofitable branch lines in the 1960s.

The essence of the scrutiny of the 'money economy' either of officials advising the Government or of simple onlookers is to judge whether any particular course of action by public bodies will result in higher interest rates or, in the austere terms of the quantity of money, a rise in the amount of money available. Public bodies provoke these pressures by seeking to borrow money for their programmes. The same, of course, is true of private individuals and bankers wishing to increase their borrowing, which will either push up interest rates or increase the supply of money.

Before looking at some of the visible signs of what is going on, a word about 'printing money'. It is often said that when the Government is presiding over an increase in the supply of money, it is 'printing money'. This is not intended to mean, as a matter of physical fact, that the presses of the printers who supply the Bank of England are running faster. What is happening is more subtle.

If the Government is spending more money than is coming in, it will borrow (more about this in chapter 8), but if that borrowing takes the form of selling more T-bills to the banks, this directly increases the supply of money. For as the Government over-spends, most of that money finds its way into the banking system as wages or payments for goods.

To cover these payments the Government sells T-bills to the banks, which have to produce money to pay for them. But in the hands of the banks, the T-bills *count as money*, and they can use the stock of such T-bills as the basis for lending to their other customers. In short, although they have lent the Government money to pay its bills, they have not got any less money themselves. The absolute quantity of money has been increased.

In this particularly murky neck of the economic woods there is no lack of signposts. As I have noted, interest rates are constantly posted by the clearing banks. The Bank of England publishes monthly the changes in the supply of money and breaks down, as best it can, the figures for bank lending to industry and to individuals for machinery, for factories or for consumer goods. When relevant, the Bank's reports, in turn reported in the press, point out changes in things like bank lending to industry or to private individuals for personal mortgages.

The money supply – the $M$ of $MV = PT$, with which I began this chapter – is itself a matter of contention. Should it be M1 (notes and coin in circulation plus current account balances at banks) or M3 (M1 plus interest-bearing deposits at banks) or other variations on the theme?

In trying to steer through the undergrowth of technical analysis and fashion, I incline to the view that changes in money comprise two elements: changes in the amount of loose cash about, which (being, roughly, M1) will rise in times either of prosperity or of inflation; and switches from the store of valuable savings into available cash, or the other way round.

In times of prosperity people will try to switch some of their M1 into M3 (otherwise known as putting something aside for a rainy day or investing for the grandchildren, according to the scale of the operation); likewise, in hard times M3 may diminish as a result of the increase of M1, as people put less aside, can afford to save less. The sorts of reason why people may do this, and the influences which bear on those decisions, are discussed in chapter 17.

At any given moment the supply of money will be influenced by these factors and another immense one: the public sector. It is the most cagey about its influence on money and interest. There are provisional figures, officially published every month, for central government borrowing and figures published quarterly for total public borrowing, which brings in the local authorities and the nationalized industries. Once a year the provisional total impact of the public spending of all government, central or local, is brought together in the White Paper on public spending. Although in recent years this crucial document has become less and less informative about future plans, it is still the single most accessible repository of information about immediate past spending by public authorities. But even this compendium of spending, past and planned, does not supply the one mesmerizing figure, the total Public Sector Borrowing Requirement (PSBR).

The importance of the PSBR is in the eye of the beholder. There has been for some years a notion that if the public sector wants to borrow more (a higher PSBR), then there will be less money for others to borrow. This is a refrain particularly favoured by those who see the only virtuous borrowing as that by private enterprise for new commercial ventures. This notion, known as 'crowding out', is contested by people (many in the City of London) who say that no one with a decent, money-making proposition has ever found it impossible to borrow because of 'crowding out' by public borrowing. The case, as they say in Scotland, is not proven (either way!).

In chasing therefore the elusive indications of the state of affairs in the money economy, watch for: interest rates, changes in money supply (especially 'real' changes after allowing for inflation), and borrowing figures, both private and public, for it is not only the government, central and local, which is always borrowing (and thus increasing the National Debt) but also private industry and individuals. Governments, of any political colour, hope not to get further into public debt. The same is true of commercial enterprises. But just as excessive borrowing sets up warning signals that managers in public service, as in private enterprise, are failing by too large a margin to make ends meet, so too little borrowing, too small an increase in credit extended and borrowings made, may be a potent sign that all is not well.

This chapter has discussed aspects of the money economy. It is the realm in which finance, borrowing and changes in the supply of money and credit are examined to measure the performance of the economy. Until fairly recently these yard-sticks were more useful, and the impact of availability of credit or money, more decisive than they seem today. Now, with the increasing complexity of the markets for money — and, in consequence, the development of more and more sources of credit and money as banks compete with building societies (see chapter 17) — and with new ways of financing schemes, from giant international loans to small personal enterprises, the tough questions about how the availability of money influences the economy seem to have softened. Controls and restrictions on national and international movements of money have gone, and the combination of high technology capable of moving money via satellite from computer to computer at will and the resourcefulness of international dealers have produced an ever-open, ever-dealing world money market.

Another aspect of modern life which makes interpretation of the money economy more difficult is the modern collapse of money itself, discussed in the next chapter on inflation.

# 5

# Inflation

What £1 would buy twenty-five years ago would now cost about £7. In the first half-dozen years of that period prices in Britain rose slowly, at less than 3 per cent a year. Then the pace began to hot up. In the dozen years 1962–74 the cost of living all but doubled. It doubled again in the next *five* years. Small wonder that after that experience Governments not only in Britain but also in the other major industrial countries where there had been similar, but less dramatic, experiences agreed that preventing such debasement of the currency must be the first priority.

Some of the consequences of these policies were described in chapter 3: the slow-down in economic activity, the rise in unemployment. At the time of writing the results are visible but modest. By mid-1982 living costs in Britain had risen a little less than 50 per cent in three years, which is less, but not a lot less, than doubling in five years. At the present rate of price increases of around 6 per cent a year, the cost of living will double again in less than a dozen years, and even at 5 per cent a year money will be halved in value in less than fifteen years.

This collapse in the value of money – the means of exchange between individuals, countries and industries – has not, however, impoverished the Western world. Living standards have not fallen by as much as living costs have risen: such a proposition would be absurd. Indeed, in most industrial countries the standard of living, whether measured by basics like housing, food and clothing, or by necessities like cars, refrigerators and washing machines, or by extras like colour television sets, foreign holidays and even *second* cars, has risen markedly over the last twenty-five years.

The insulation of the population from the effects of inflation is as obvious as the nose on your face: wages or other earnings have kept up with rising prices for most of the time, except when rising faster. Periods when 'real earnings' – that is, people's incomes after adjusting for rising prices – have actually fallen, have been rare in the last quarter-century.

Inflation, then, has gone hand-in-hand with rising prosperity in the post-war period. And yet there is a widespread and scarcely questioned view that it is a thoroughly bad thing and that governments should make sustained efforts to stamp out inflation. On the other hand, there is also a strong body of argument that the efforts to prevent inflation can produce results which are worse than the affliction of rising prices. Later on in this chapter I shall discuss how inflation affects different groups in society – wage-earners, pensioners, entrepreneurs and the like – but first a quick general look at this question: which is worse, inflation or the attempts to cure it?

The greatest damage that inflation does in general is to remove from the economic scene the certainty provided by a stable currency. This has immediate and obvious effects on commercial and private life. When the future value of money is not known, people are not so ready to take risks and engage in the experiments and commercial ventures which, in times of stable prices, have contributed enormously to growing prosperity. When the value of the counters in the game are constantly changing, the players are inhibited.

But what about the cures for inflation? Conventionally, these are the 'stops' in 'stop-go' policies: higher taxation, credit squeezes and a slowing down in the size of price increases and wage settlements, either with or without formal incomes policies. In either case economic policies designed to slow down inflation invariably slow down real economic activity as well. The reason for this is that it is well-nigh impossible to introduce policies which inhibit *only* price rises. To take an example: compulsory price controls forbidding suppliers from putting up their prices may briefly hold the price level down, but if the price level held is too low, then suppliers will simply drop out of that type of business, and real economic activity, as well as the target of prices, will be affected. On a large scale this means that 'squeeze' policies, whether higher taxation, higher interest rates or other controls, invariably produce higher unemployment while also slowing down the rate of inflation.

One of the most persistent worries for economic policy-makers in recent years has been that as inflation has got worse (as described at the start of this chapter), so the attempts to 'cure' inflation have seemed to have smaller effects on inflation and greater effects on the real level of economic activity, pushing unemployment and economic stagnation to worse and worse levels. Why, then, persist in the ungrateful task of trying to halt inflation, if in broad, general terms everyone has been jogging along, getting slightly better off, with only occasional hiccups? What is all the fuss about? In one sense, perhaps there is too much fuss. Perhaps an essential part of making sense of the economy is not to get too dramatic about it. Perhaps it does not matter if prices rise a bit faster as long as wages and earnings keep up.

That is not the view of politicians or economists. Karl Marx himself advised that a useful first step to revolution was to 'debauch the currency'. Without being so apocalyptic, many others have felt the same thing. It is a deeply and profoundly held view in Western economic societies that money is not just the 'medium of exchange' between consumers and suppliers, the reward for labour which can then be spent on beer, baccy or Old Master paintings. Money is much more than that: it seems to be the very store of value, the means of transmission of virtue and of comfort among members of society, whether the money-lender in a rural Indian village or the first Duke of Marlborough with his newly built palace outside Woodstock, named Blenheim after his most famous victory.

In spite of the fact that money itself has *no* value, except what people will exchange it for, it has great psychological importance, and tampering with money is a deadly sin. Consider the furore when Britain 'went decimal'. There are a great many people – not excluding my wife – who lay at the door of the Decimal Currency Board and of the Government which allowed its recommendations to take effect the blame for recent inflation. In dry statistical terms this is evidently nonsense. The sevenfold rise in prices in the last twenty-five years was influenced by not more than the tiniest jot by the switch from the sensible duodecimal system of pounds, shillings and pence to the Napoleonic relic of decimal coinage. (I call the duodecimal system sensible because a shilling, or twelve pence, could be divided, without fractions, by four different numbers, 2, 3, 4 and 6. A decimal unit can be divided precisely by only two, 2 and 5. If only God had given us six fingers to a hand, we could still be enjoying the infinitely greater arithmetic flexibility of the duodecimal, rather than the decimal system.)

However, the actual impact on prices of the change was slight in relation to other forces afoot. This can be demonstrated both by the fact that other countries, where there was no change analogous to decimalization, experienced equal catastrophes in relation to the value of their currencies, and by the sorry tale that the worst period for inflation in Britain was not the period spanning decimalization but the horrendous mid-1970s.

But that is not to say that old wives' tales and instincts are wrong. In a sense any attack on the currency is an attack on stability, on accepted values, on what people believe is the 'right' price to pay. In this sense decimalization was certainly an undermining of confidence in the High Street analogous to the undermining of confidence in the international scene when President Nixon devalued the dollar – and broke the final vestigial link between money and gold – in 1971. I shall come back to this fundamental and profoundly upsetting change in the post-war world, but for the moment I shall only say that it was a retreat from stability likely to add to inflation, not to ease it.

General de Gaulle, President of France, evidently shared the British shopper's distrust of change and respect for money when, after a crisis meeting in Germany, the Finance Ministers of the major powers agreed in the summer of 1967 that the French franc should be devalued by about 15 per cent. This happened on Friday night, too late for Saturday's morning papers in London. But next day economic and political experts working for the Sunday papers had plenty of time to compose articles describing the devaluation in detail and drawing enjoyable and detailed pictures of 'France after devaluation'.

All except for one editor, the late Patrick Hutber of the *Sunday Telegraph*. Even as the French functionaries led by the Finance Minister sped back from Germany to the Élysée Palace and President de Gaulle, Patrick Hutber held back his pen. As he said to me afterwards, 'I thought to myself, if you were called President de Gaulle, and your country was France, and your currency was called the franc, would you devalue?' He was the only one who was right, of course. De Gaulle's instinct was to reject such debasement. He subscribed to the mythical power of tradition. The European powers were told that the franc would stay where it was, and the English Sunday papers had to lump it.

These reflections are prompted by the difficulty of getting to grips with the question 'So what's wrong with inflation?'. It is a question which must be mastered if the workings of the economy and the influences on decision taking are to be approached, let alone answered. For a President of France at one end of the scale and the casual shopper distrustful of new and changed coinage at the other there is the common dislike of moving from the known to the unknown and, by implication, from the disciplines of a present system to the relative anarchy of the novel.

But what of the consequences of sharply rising prices for the various elements in a modern society? At a first glance inflation in the modern world might be thought to favour the wage-earner because his income, give or take a little, is tied to the 'cost of living' and will rise as fast as prices, while the *rentier*, the entrepreneur, or the self-employed may not be able to increase his income as fast. Reflection quickly shows that the answer is not so simple. The *rentier*, owning bricks and mortar or shares in companies, may not see his income rise as fast as prices at a time of sharp inflation, but as, in consequence, the value of money falls, the value of his possessions will rise. Income may be dented, but wealth will be protected by the very mechanism of inflation itself.

The entrepreneur always lives relatively dangerously, making deals, buying and selling and doing well by anticipation. To him inflation is just another factor to be coped with, neither especially threatening nor advantageous.

It has always been emphasized that the group of people who suffer most from inflation are those on relatively fixed incomes. The classic case is the pensioner whose pension is not protected against rising prices and has no way of earning more income. Because of this very clear and simple evil of inflation, the state pension has, for most of the period of recent rapid inflation, been increased faster than the rise in living costs. That does not mean that all pensioners are better off, for many enjoy two pensions: their small but protected state entitlement, and their own occupational pension, or savings, which may not be protected at all. That is one reason why the inflation-linked pensions of civil servants have attracted the disparaging envy of many people: in spite of the fact that Civil Service pensions, though protected against rising prices, are relatively mean by comparison with those of other career professionals in similar trades.

Each individual will decide whether he loses or gains by inflation in his personal life (see chapter 17). There are wider consequences for the community at large. Perhaps the most important of these is not the absolute decline in the value of money but the increasing disparity between rates of inflation in different countries.

The great economic evil of inflation may be not to suffer rising prices but to watch your prices rise faster than the other fellow's. It is certainly true that in the last twenty-five years as the average rate of inflation for all countries has accelerated violently, so the variation between countries has also increased.

In the 'old days' – say, the 1950s and 1960s – it was rare for rates of inflation anywhere in the industrial West to be more than 2 or 3 per cent a year. Within those bands one country might do 1 or 2 per cent a year better or worse than another. In the late 1970s in Western Europe alone the range of national rates of inflation was from 5 per cent in Germany, through 10 per cent in Britain, to 13 per cent in France and nearly 20 per cent in Italy.

The consequences for the prosperity of all these countries, depending to a greater or lesser extent on their foreign trading with one another and with third parties, is clearly linked to their inflation rates. This great breadth of differences is in some respects the most frightening aspect of inflation. Everyone wants to be the least expensive supplier so as to get the best share of the market. It is the other side of the coin of competitiveness to maintain the lowest rate of inflation, the most consistent selling prices. At the same time all governments hark back to the days, for all of them, of relatively stable prices.

To follow the latest turns in inflation there is no shortage of information. The Department of Employment produces, once a month, the General Index of Retail Prices, and there is also something called the Tax and Prices Index (TPI), published with some embarrassment by the Central Statistical Office, which purports to show the impact on the family of changes in both prices and taxes. The trouble with the TPI is that while it was designed to show that you are as well off if income tax is cut as if value-added tax (VAT) is cut (and VAT changes are reflected in the Retail Price Index, though personal taxes are not), the difficulty of constructing a cross-section of the tax-paying public who would be representative of the whole has not been met. The Retail Price Index (RPI) may contain anomalies (as, for instance, the fact that both interest charges on mortgages and the level of council house rents are included, yet precious few people *both* live in a council house *and* have a mortgage), but it is by far the most reliable general indicator of what is happening to prices.

Be warned, however, about reading it. The most frequently quoted figure derived from the monthly RPI is often called 'the annual rate of inflation'. It is no such thing. If there were an 'annual rate of inflation', it could, I suppose, be derived from looking at a number of years' price increases and then dividing the whole by the number of years to get a 'rate'. But this vital figure that is so often quoted is actually the amount of the rise in the index over the previous twelve months. To discover a 'rate', and therefore to get a sensible view of what is going on, it is much better to look at the changes in prices in the index over a few months, always allowing for the sort of special factors described in chapter 2.

Newspapers do a reasonable job reporting the RPI, but each has its own approach, and there is no substitute for the raw figures. These are published once a month by press notice from the Department of Employment. The press notice gives a run of six months for the main figures – the index, the index excluding seasonal food, the movements over three months and six months – and a breakdown of the most recent changes into finer categories: housing, fuel, tobacco, meals out and so on. For greater detail the best source, though the figures are bound to be a month late, is the invaluable monthly *Digest of Statistics*, published by the Stationary Office and available in good public reference libraries. All you need is a pocket calculator, since the *Digest* does not give, as the press notice does, the percentage changes.

The RPI is important, not least because it has become the yardstick on which wage claims are often based. But it is not the only measure of inflation. Attempts to seek a broader view of price changes, not just those affecting the consumer, have resulted in the 'deflator', a tool of national accounting which tries to turn the actual figures for national income into 'real' figures by excluding the effect of price changes.

Moving further afield, the Organization for Economic Co-operation and Development (OECD) in Paris publishes once a month the latest movements in consumer prices in the main OECD countries, a convenient guide to how the main Western industrial countries are vying with each other to keep inflation in check.

And a step or so behind the final figures are what are called, for convenience, 'wholesale prices'. These figures, prepared by the Department of Industry, are in fact, two series. They chart both the prices paid by industry for raw materials and fuel arriving at the factory and the prices at which products move out. These industrial prices can act as early warning if another burst of price increases to consumers is in the pipeline and equally show when there is at least one element (material costs) which is not going up.

While industrial prices give a rough and ready guide to what is likely to happen to inflation, they form only one small part of the picture, for, as Sir Arthur (now Lord) Cockfield, accountant, civil servant and Minister of the Crown, once observed to me at his office in the Prices Commission, about 85 per cent of all costs are, directly or indirectly, wage costs.

# 6

# Wages

It was, if I remember right, the late Lord Feather – Vic Feather of the TUC – who once said, 'A pay rise of 5 per cent when prices are rising at 3 per cent is better, far better, than a rise of 15 per cent when prices were rising at 13 per cent.' The difficulty is that if Lord Cockfield is right, and 85 per cent of costs are, directly or indirectly, labour costs, then wages chasing prices – or more especially, as in Vic Feather's example, keeping ahead of prices – are themselves bound to push prices further up. It is classic chicken-and-egg territory and one of the most puzzling features of the economy for observers to deal with.

Wages cannot be taken in isolation: they have come to form the lynchpin of a series of economic relations which includes prices, unemployment, profits and national prosperity. And within what we call wages in general there are the fierce tensions and battles of 'relativities' and 'differentials'. Furthermore, throughout the debate on the importance of wages in the economy, a very sharp eye must be kept on the difference between 'money wages' and 'real wages'. At the time of writing, for instance, Government Ministers are insisting that for the long-run prosperity of the country and recovery from the recession, 'wages must fall'. They mean real wages, not money wages. They mean that by accepting in pay packets increases that are smaller than the rise in living costs, British wage-earners will be making themselves more competitive and therefore more likely to succeed in future. They do not mean that wage-earners in general should take a cut in the pay packet itself, though in a handful of private firms some workers have accepted lower money wages when the alternative was a shut-down and no wages at all.

Charting the course of wages is much more difficult than following price developments. There are a number of distinct sources. First, there are the officially gathered statistics for the whole economy. The Department of Employment publishes monthly figures for basic wage rates, but, as the label suggests, these basic rates are usually less than most people receive. More reliable as a guide to the way things are going, but sometimes difficult to interpret, is the index of average earnings.

Average earnings include payments for overtime (or reductions for short-time), and the index reflects back pay when a settlement is backdated. The difficulty about reading the average earnings index is that for most people wage increases tend to come but once a year, while the index is charted every month. Each month, however, it is affected by the settlements made in the previous four weeks or back pay and by changes in patterns of work (over- or short-time). For this reason probably the only sensible use to which the index can be put is to make annual comparisons: even quarterly changes will be heavily weighted by settlements or, in certain fallow times of the year, by a complete absence of settlements to nudge the index in any direction.

What the earnings watcher can do is to see how the annual comparison is changing month by month, up or down, but even that can lead to false conclusions, since a month with few settlements may produce a low figure for annual comparison, which is quickly overtaken a month later when a hefty settlement in the public sector has gone through.

For this reason other, almost anecdotal evidence is worth seeking. The CBI runs a 'databank' of pay settlements; its members notify headquarters of the deals they have agreed and thus enable the CBI to keep track of the sorts of award being made by commercial and industrial companies.

When it comes to the public sector, the railwaymen, miners, nurses, electrical power workers and dustmen, there is no shortage of information about the size of their wage increases, for in the recent past the amount they have been paid has been widely proclaimed, whether in terms extolling the victory of a campaign for higher wages or as an acknowledgement of an acceptable offer, reasonably accepted.

It should not, therefore, be difficult to pick up the rudiments of the way in which wages and earnings are moving. What is much more difficult – at the heart, as I have already suggested, of the economic conundrum of Britain – is where they *should* be going. To make sense of the economy as it confronts us, there is the simple question: are we paying ourselves too much? Is it the case that we have set wage and earning levels at a pitch which will meet the expectations of those who draw wages or earn livings but will make the product of their efforts so dear that they do not sell?

For about three-quarters of the product of Britain the buyers are the same people (or their relations) as those involved in the production. The wife complaining about the higher price of bread may be complaining to her husband, the power worker, who has just been awarded a pay rise that is even larger, in percentage terms, than the rise in the price of bread. And if she cross-questions the baker, he might blame his higher electricity bills for the higher price of a loaf. In which case she might retort sharply, 'Don't blame my husband. We've àll got to live, haven't we?'

There are two distinct points to make about the movement of wages as they effect the economic argument – and, indeed, beyond the simple economic field. The first was encapsulated for me when an editor once warned me, at a time of high and growing inflation, that higher wages, were never bad news, however much disparaged by economists, I have come latterly to disagree with his judgement: higher wages may well be bad news for those who, drawing them for a few weeks or months, suddenly find themselves out of a job altogether because the price of the product or service has had to reflect the rise in wages. This might be called 'pricing yourself out of the market'.

The second point, much more common, much more vigorous, is 'keeping up with the Joneses', and it has a profound effect on contemporary economists. The point was exceptionally well put, in a report from the Pay Board set up by the Conservative Government of 1970–4, that the relatively low pay of groups of workers like dustmen or nurses could not be improved in purchasing power, or real terms, without the consent of those who earned more to *being caught up*. If we want to see nurses getting a better deal, the report implied, than those with more ingrained strength, muscle and better money for the job must allow the pay of nurses (and hospital porters, and dustmen) to creep up. For, this sensible report argued, if every skilled union or closed shop insisted on maintaining 'historic differentials', then all pay would rise *pro rata* and, as the consequent rise in living costs came along, the nurses would be at the bottom again!

There is, of course, the contrary argument that in the hard world of economic reality the least well paid are least well paid because that's what they are 'worth'. If nurses and dustmen are badly paid, it is because other people would rush in to fill every opening left by disgruntled dustmen or nurses who left their jobs for lack of money.

There are, in consequence, warring factions in all talk about proper wages. The same people who complain that they cannot find a window cleaner or depend on a decent car service at their local garage protest vehemently at the charge of £2 or £10 an hour for labour.

But on the whole the battleground over wages has moved away from small merchants and individual deals to the heavy forum of free collective bargaining, where trade unions or associations of trade unions meet employers and wrestle.

It is virtually impossible to assess, at a casual glance, who is right in any row over a pay claim. For the trade union the starting-point may be, 'We want at least enough to keep up with rising prices and a bit more because we are splendid and loyal workers – and if we don't get it, watch it!' While the employers say, 'We're losing money on everything you people help to make, so we can't afford to pay more than we can justify by greater efficiency, which might mean lower prices and higher sales. Otherwise there'll be redundancies.'

There is a much nastier complication when the employer is the public sector: mines, steel, railways, the Post Office, the Civil Service, hospitals or schools. Then the argument parodied above becomes even sharper because the employees feel that in striving for higher living standards they are struggling not only against the immediate employer – British Rail, the Coal Board, the local health authority – but also against the Government itself which, whether Labour or Conservative, has an explicit or implicit incomes policy designed to do them down. The recent past is littered with cases in which, openly or otherwise, trade unions in the public sector have 'taken on' the Government as well as the individual employer. It is understandable that both sides dislike the fact that the ultimate paymaster is also the referee.

Another aspect of the Government's role in wage bargaining is the vexed question of formal incomes policies. Disliked by both employers and employees, these are most criticized by economists and politicians, who argue that after a year or two of restraint such policies crumble or are abandoned, and there is a wave of 'catching up' which makes the last state worse than the first. This, I believe, is a political phenomenon. Thus in 1974–5, after the Labour Party successes in the elections, the Pay Board and Ted Heath's third year of incomes policy were abandoned for political reasons and a 'social contract' was substituted which led to very large increases in money wages indeed. There was no economic justification at all for this, and by Christmas 1974 the Labour Chancellor, Denis Healey, was warning the trade unions that if they persisted with large pay settlements, he would 'take it back' in the spring Budget. As we saw in chapter 1, that is just what he did.

At the end of that Government in 1979, the surge of wage awards after three years' restraint and the 'winter of discontent', were formally institutionalized in the famous Clegg Commission, which was given powers to enable public service workers to 'catch up' with other workers. The Conservative Government which inherited the Clegg pledges for the 1979 pay round blamed on that surge many of their own troubles with inflation the following year. And while forswearing formal incomes policy, the Conservative administration adopted a pretty tough incomes policy of its own by the autumn of 1980 when it announced a limit of 7 per cent on the amount of money available to increase pay in the public sector.

The objections to incomes policies are several: few of them are strictly economic. Apart from the wave effect just touched on, there is the unpleasing truth that, to be any good, incomes policies should be a tightening screw, not a short, sharp shock. Thus if the aim of policy is to reduce inflation, to reverse the horrifying trend set out in the last chapter, then each successive rise in money wages should be smaller than the one before. In theory, that will produce slower price increases, so that at the end of the day 'real' wages are not reduced, and Vic Feather's desirable goal is reached.

The trouble often is that the desired end, small price increases, is not delivered by the undoubted sacrifice of limited money wage increases now. For example, though not a formal incomes policy, the Conservative experiment in limiting cash available for public-sector pay went: 1980 7 per cent, 1981 4 per cent and 1982 nil! The nil was not an official figure, but it was what the Chancellor of the Exchequer, Sir Geoffrey Howe, publicly proclaimed in a speech as desirable 'in an ideal world'.

The Conservative experiment – which did see a fall in the rate of inflation from over 20 to under 6 per cent a year – also attempted to demonstrate the link between wages and employment. In setting the 7 per cent and 4 per cent ceilings on money for public-sector pay, the Government made no stipulation about the size of wage settlements. If employers and work force agreed on a pay rise more than that, they would have to find the money by reducing the labour force. The results were a compromise: wage settlements were generally above the ceiling; some jobs were lost; and the total wage bills rose by only slightly more than the Government's two ceilings. It is virtually certain that both total wage bills and absolute levels of pay rose much less than they would have without the policy.

Other periods of incomes policy have been either more, or less, successful. Among objections to them one of the most serious for economists is that they distort the labour market. It is argued that wage rates should be untrammelled so that if demand for a particular kind of work rises, people should be drawn to it by higher wages offered there. If another activity is getting old hat, people should be paid less in real terms so that they seek work elsewhere. To conservative trade unionists and others this may seem a harsh view of life. There are many who argue 'once a coalminer, always a coalminer'. But, in truth, such changes are happening the whole time. The steel industry in Britain has contracted sharply just as the North Sea oil industry has expanded. And while in real terms steelworkers' pay may have fallen, very high wages have been offered, and taken, for the hazardous, uncomfortable, sometimes boring but always well paid work on the oil rigs.

It is also argued that a regime of incomes policies under which everyone receives the same pay award freezes the economic map at a point which may – nay, certainly will – be the wrong shape in one, two or three years' time.

Translating the 'moving picture' of demand for new skills – the changes in job patterns – into practical help is something I will touch on in Part III, where individual choices and decisions are examined. It is difficult for the job-seeker, whether trying to enter the labour force (from school or college) or trying to find a new job after losing one, to know what new work is around the corner. In chapter 18 the role of Jobcentres, training schemes and just plain gossip will be discussed as signposts in a world where both opportunities and pay rates are changing all the time.

On the national, if not the personal, level there is plenty of evidence of these changes in relative pay, charted in Government figures for rates of pay in different trades, occupations and professions. The Department of Employment *Gazette* gives fuller details than the monthly *Digest of Statistics*, but both can be used to monitor the changing shape of wage patterns in the country. They also show the number of hours worked on average in industry, and this will become one of the central arguments about wages in the near future.

Confronted with the prospect of high unemployment for years to come, the labour movement in Britain and elsewhere has been casting around for ways to mitigate the curse of unemployment. One fashionable runner has become the shorter working week. The goal of no more than thirty-five hours as the basic week – instead of forty or even forty-two – has been announced by many labour organizations.

The snag, which employers or their organizations like the CBI have been quick to point out, is that this shorter working week must not be allowed to add to the wage bill per unit of output. That, they argue, would be to add to costs and prices, with a consequent loss of sales and then, perhaps, the loss of far more jobs than shorter working could provide. Therefore, it is argued, if a shorter working week is introduced as a means to reduce unemployment, the existing labour force must share with the jobless not only its work but also its money. If trade unions agree that the larger labour force which might be taken on directly through fewer working hours would receive *the same total wages*, and therefore less per man, then the scheme would be feasible. At the moment there is still firm resistance to any measures which would cut the pay of individual workers. From this apparent deadlock it is hard to see what will emerge: this is a wage issue which will run and run.

One reason why such national issues as the shorter working week or the impact of high money wage settlements on employment are so difficult to resolve is that, being essentially large-scale, they do not loom large in the priorities of wage-bargainers. Just as an employer may use devices like extra perks or allowances to attract workers in defiance of a national incomes policy (thereby weakening it), so individual wage negotiators are unlikely to pay much heed to the overall economic strategy, leaving that argument to Government and the economic committee of the TUC.

It was a former chairman of the TUC who put it to me, when I was discussing the relation of jobs and wages, that no trade union negotiator could, or even should, take the broader national interest into account when driving a wage bargain for his members. It was not what he was elected for. And though he was a moderate in national affairs, he believed that trade union negotiators should press for the best possible deal for their workers. To do less would be to let them down, especially if others, perhaps with more muscle, were doing better, even if this was against the wider national interest and might add to unemployment. One of his colleagues in the movement, of a harder-nosed variety, added this chilling rider: why, when driving a hard bargain for his members, should he concern himself with unemployment? The unemployed were not in his union.

This single-minded pursuit of higher wages, carried out throughout the economy by sectional interests for their own members, is another aspect of the economic scene which will be of enormous importance in shaping the future prosperity of the country.

# 7

# Productivity

'We on Merseyside have got big hearts,' said the MP for a Liverpool constituency, as he thumped his chest in emphasis, 'and that's why none of our lads would do anything in the factory which might so much as threaten anyone else's job.'

We had been talking for more than an hour about the closure of a biggish plant on Merseyside, much resented by the MP and his colleagues but arising from the fact that productivity in this plant was far lower than elsewhere in the industry. In the face of over-supply of the products made there, something had to be closed, and the poor record of output per man in this case decided the factory's fate.

One of the managing directors at the table responded. 'You have put it better than any of us could,' he told the MP. 'It is because no one at the factory would co-operate to increase productivity that in the end not some but *all* of the jobs there have gone.'

That snatch of dialogue between a local MP and the management of the company which had invited him in to explain the closure of the works points up the crucial dilemma at the heart of industry's performance. Management, understandably, wants the highest possible productivity. Only with high output per man can it reduce unit costs, and then compete with other companies, either by selling more at lower prices or by earning high returns on what it does sell. And for this, it feels acutely the need for acceptance by the labour force of new techniques and the best use of the new investments it makes in modern equipment. It is a paradox that spokesmen for the labour force in the trade union movement often berate management for not investing enough, while entrenched labour practices mean that the investment itself is sabotaged.

In the case of the very factory over whose demise we were arguing there had been just such an affair. The managers had invested in a new machine for checking finished products before they left the factory, which could work three times as fast as the previous model. This investment of tens of thousands of pounds was then rendered virtually useless by the decision of the men not to increase the output of the testing bay. As a result the machine was used for twenty minutes, then left idle for twice that time before it resumed work. While nothing had been done to threaten anyone else's job, at the same time the hard-earned money which management had set aside for the new, more efficient machine had been virtually torn up in its face by labour practice.

The frustrations on both sides in this sort of affair reflect differences of view about what industry is for. From the outside, industry, all economic activity, can be seen either as the arrangements that societies make to provide citizens with the goods and standard of living they expect or as the provider of employment so that the same members of society have both an occupation and the wherewithal to pay for the products of industry and energy.

The entrepreneurs and managers, the businessmen who 'run' industry, see their part of the battlefield rather differently. They have a narrower view, based on whatever product or service they are making and selling. For them one of the most important objectives is to compete successfully with rivals doing the same thing. Seeing things from closer to, as the manager must, he is more concerned with the relationship between his enterprise and the customer and therefore will want to maximize efficiency, sales and profits; he is perhaps less concerned with the grand overall view of the economy.

On the other hand, there are those in trade unions, in local trades councils and in politics who see industry as providing prosperity for their members or their constituents. Not only locally but also nationally, organizations are prepared to compete to increase the number of jobs in their patch, even if at the expense of others. Later on we'll come to trade wars and protectionism (in chapter 13), but the tug of war between those competing for jobs and those competing for efficiency often turns on productivity itself.

It is not the easiest thing in the economy to chart, though it is one of the most important. The simplest way of examining productivity is to take the two components of which it is made and to match them up. This means monitoring the absolute level of output of this or that industry or of the whole economy and then assessing, with the aid of the unemployment figures, what changes there have been in the manpower contributing to that output.

This is all very well for industries like steel, in which tonnes produced can be directly compared with the numbers working to arrive at output per head, but much more difficult when it comes to services like education, health, welfare or such things as TV and show business.

For one thing, productivity may have a greater value in some activities than in others. The productivity of a teacher with a class of forty secondary-school pupils is clearly higher, in crude terms, than that of one with twenty or even fifteen pupils. But few people would contest that the classroom with the smaller number of pupils provides the better education. In manufacturing, on the other hand, there would be few to argue that higher output per head, and therefore both cheaper goods and easier working conditions for the labour force itself, were desirable. In between, perhaps, are enterprises like shops, where complete abandonment to self-service may produce cheaper grocery bills but also, for some customers, irritation or frustration that outweigh the economies of higher productivity.

In general, the importance of productivity in industry is directly related to competition. (It is possible, and sometimes desirable, to have low productivity; but that is invariably coupled with low wages and some sort of protection, national or local, or policies of employment maximization). To make

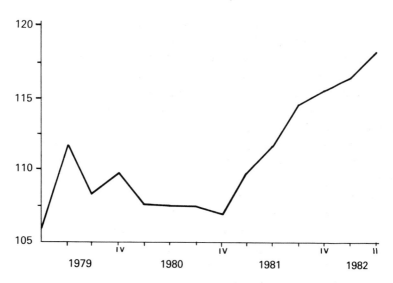

*The decline in productivity (output per man hour) from mid-1979 to late 1980 reflected a fall in industry's output that was faster than the decline in the work force. From then on the very sharp rise in unemployment – and redundancies, mostly in manufacturing industry – meant that output per man hour rose as the number of those employed fell.*

Source: Central Statistical Office, *Economic Trends*, London, HMSO, various issues.

*Figure 2  Productivity: manufacturing output per man hour, 1979–82 (index 1975 = 100)*

sense of what is happening to productivity, and therefore whether a change in productivity is good news or the reverse, it is helpful to know the background to changes in output per man-hour.

For instance, there was considerable controversy during the 1980–2 slump about the change in productivity in British industry. Undoubtedly, the output of manufacturing, and of the economy as a whole, did not fall as sharply as the fall in employment. The simple inference was that productivity was rising, and some politicians, such as the Prime Minister and

Chancellor of the Exchequer, emphasized the progress which this represented.

Others took a different view: that efficiency was not rising in industry; that while some plants and factories were closing down for good (and taking with them a higher proportion of jobs than of output), those industries that survived were not very much more efficient: and that if there were a recovery in output, there would be an immediate reassertion of old, bad habits, and productivity would fall. Almost certainly there is truth on both sides of this argument: and even if some factories were lost for good, taking more jobs with them than their share of output, that very fact meant that it was the least efficient who were failing, and that those that remained would be, as the Prime Minister said, 'leaner and fitter'.

So much for the controversy over productivity in recession. It is a useful rule of thumb to have in the back of one's mind that productivity will tend to rise late on during a down-turn, and early on during an up-turn. This is because, in general, employers do not like losing workers. Even as their sales fall or profit margins come under pressure, they will tend to hold on to the people they employ. Overtime may be reduced, short-time working come in, but only when the going has been rough for some time will employers begin to lay off and fire workers permanently – and that is the moment when productivity rises fairly sharply.

Conversely, when some sort of recovery arrives and sales begin to rise, employers are keen not to increase their payroll and staff until absolutely necessary. They find that they can get on quite well during the initial phases of recovery with the same labour force, and for this reason general figures for unemployment often go on rising for months after total output has begun to increase.

At the other end of the cycle – that is to say, towards the end of the up-turn and the beginning of the down-turn – increases in productivity are less likely. Towards the end of any boom employment will be rising as fast as output, and often new firms, bringing with them new staffs and payrolls, will be entering the field. And as we have seen, when the down-turn starts, employers are reluctant to let go their workers, so that for some months, with output static or falling, there is no change in numbers employed, and productivity remains flat or falls.

These changes in output per man (or per man-hour) are influenced by the business cycle of growth and pause (or recession) and then resumed growth. Even more important may be long-run changes in productivity in different countries and industries.

Major changes in national productivity for the whole economy tend to happen when workers are moving on a large scale from one kind of work to another, more mechanized field of work. The classic cases of increased productivity are, for instance, the eighteenth-, nineteenth- and twentieth-century migrations of workers from the land to the towns and cities, from agriculture to mechanical industry (which also increased productivity on the land, as machines replaced the people who had gone to the towns); the famous introduction of the assembly line by Henry Ford; and now the large-scale appearance in manufacturing industry of micro-processors and robotics.

The phenomenon of productivity – which is the reverse of the coin of human inventiveness and enterprise – poses especially awkward questions in the later part of the twentieth century. Just at a time when world demand is sluggish, the emergent nations of the poorer world are beginning to scent the rewards of higher productivity, while the mature industrial economies, which have enjoyed the advances provided by higher productivity for more than the last fifty years, are feeling nervous about the effect of higher productivity (because of cheap labour) in the competing countries like Korea, Pakistan, the Philippines, now emerging to join Japan among the challengers to the old European and North American industrial countries. At the same time, in a world apparently all too well supplied with competing goods and services, the very improvements in productivity and technology which are vital to the competitive success of the mature industrial countries threaten to increase idleness and unemployment among their citizens.

Increased productivity – for those who are achieving it – is an unmixed blessing only when the final demand for the goods produced is rising. Given a static or growing potential labour force, higher output per man is all very well if there is also growing output in total; but if that is not the case, the problem is different. In his Budget speech for 1982 the Chancellor of the Exchequer forecast a growth of 1 per cent in national output in the coming year (and felt that was a 'good thing' after the decline of the year before). He also spoke of output per man rising at a considerably faster rate than that. (He was pleased about that too, as it showed that industry was using its manpower better.) But put those two plusses together and the simple, inexorable arithmetic of output per man rising considerably faster than output in total signals higher unemployment. Sir Geoffrey Howe did not spell that out in his Budget speech, but then the monthly figures for the out-of-work in succeeding months did it very clearly for him.

# 8

# Public Spending

More than one working person in three in Britain works for government, central or local, or for a state industry. This, the public sector, spends just about half of every penny or pound spent in the United Kingdom each year. In 1983 the cost of this vast enterprise will be more than £5,000 per household, and for working people the average impost is higher, more like £6,000 per head in one year alone. And all this money has to come from tax and government borrowing.

This means that close on half of the money earned by average earners flows, one way or another, through the public sector – be it in rates or rents to local councils, national insurance contributions for pensions and the health service or taxes on income and spending to pay for everything from the civil servants in Whitehall and elsewhere to new motorways and railway electrification.

It is not surprising that public spending is one of the most urgently debated economic issues in the land. One reason for this is that on the part of those who pay there is really no choice about how the money is spent. Electorates may throw out Governments – and, typically, before an election one side will say that it wants to spend more, the other that it wants to spend less, so that the voter may feel he is voting in effect for more or less government spending. But when the dust of the election has settled, whichever side assumes power will continue to spend almost exactly as much on hospitals, on defence, on social services and the like as did its predecessor. There is, equally, very little room for manoeuvre among those who spend the money. Old habits (and new ones) die hard, and the spending Departments of government cling resolutely to their programmes and projects, whether the spender is a local town hall providing road sweepers and meals-on-wheels or a great Department of state funding aircraft carriers and nuclear weapons.

Apart from this very strong inertia, which carries every sort of spending programme forward with great force, there is another aspect of public spending which makes it especially difficult to control. This is well exemplified in an American method of explaining to people how their tax dollars are spent. The Americans divide all public spending into mandatory and discretionary expenditures. When things like state retirement pensions, unemployment benefit and, in Britain, family income supplement, child benefit and supplementary benefits, are totted up, it turns out that these state commitments to pay – whatever happens to state income – amount to a substantial sum of money. Then there are equally binding legal obliga- tions: for instance, the duties laid on local authorities to pro- vide education through state schools up to a certain standard and age for all children, and the provision of the National Health Service, with its hospitals, general practice and the whole range of health visitors and special services.

These public services are prescribed by law: and they cost a good deal more than half the total of public spending. The rest – defence, diplomacy through the Foreign and Comonwealth Office, housing, roads, transport, the nationalized industries – are the areas in which the Government of the day has the power to economize without reneging not just on past hopes but also on the law of the land.

In recent years Governments of both parties have been trying not only to manage public spending but also to improve their techniques for controlling it. The most significant changes have been the adoption of cash limits under the 1974–9 Labour Government and a refinement, cash planning, under the Conservatives.

In essence, until the mid-1970s public spending was largely planned on the basis of programmes. We will, the planners

*Table 2 Public spending: shares of expenditure, 1982–3 (%)*

| Area of expenditure | Percentage of total |
| --- | --- |
| Social security | 29 |
| Defence | 13 |
| Health | 12 |
| Education | 11 |
| Industry | 5 |
| Roads and transport | 4 |
| Law and order | 4 |
| Housing | 2 |
| Remainder | 20 |

*Social security payments, provision for health and monies for education, which are largely obligatory under the law, occupied three of the first four places in the public expenditure league table in 1982–3 and accounted for more than half of the total of more than £113,000 millions. In this and any other fiscal year, therefore, the only major savings to be made are in defence, transport and support for industry, and in these areas successive Governments exercise considerable discretion.*

Source: HM Treasury, *White Paper on Public Expenditure*, Cmnd 8789, London, HMSO, 1983.

decided, be able to afford so many hospitals, so many miles of motorway, so much for the Army or the Navy. Once the programmes were agreed, they proceeded. Sometimes the agencies carrying out the programmes under-spent (usually through inefficiency – the work was just not organized quickly enough), but far more often the cost of programmes turned out to be much higher than anticipated, and with inflation accelerating in all aspects of life, the bill for an agreed set of public works in particular always turned out to be far larger than the plan.

In response to this fact of inflationary life, the Treasury introduced the concept of cash limits. This simply meant that once a programme of work had been agreed, it could go forward, but if it cost more than planned, then work must be stopped or controlled to keep within the cash limit for the year in question. In essence, instead of saying, 'You may build ten hospitals, whatever the cost', the new rules said, 'You may build ten hospitals and here is £x million for that purpose. Once you've spent the £x million, you stop, even if you haven't completed ten hospitals.' The refinement of cash planning is a tool to show future spending plans in cash rather than in programme terms: not so many schools, but so much money to spend on schools.

These devices were only part of the efforts made by governments to control spending. Governments also try to save money by changing the laws of the land. Successive Finance Bills passed to carry out the intention of Budgets have, for instance, changed the rules of family allowances (substituting child benefit, a cash payment, for allowances against tax) or introducing increases in benefits that are less than enough to pay for higher living costs.

But, as a general rule, in the 1980s the Government faces a juggernaut of public spending which looms very large indeed in its economic planning but is very difficult substantially to change.

To make sense of the continuous arguments over government and other public spending, a number of different approaches are required. First, there is the need to discover what is currently going on. Then there is the question, touched on above, of examining the room to manoeuvre – that is, how governments can change public spending (usually how they can cut it back). Thirdly, there is the important issue of the way in which the state of the whole economy affects public spending.

There is plenty of available information about public spending. Once a year the Government publishes a White Paper announcing its intentions for the years ahead and outlining the spending of the immediate past. The detail varies enormously, not only according to the decisions of Government about what to provide in the way of future plans but also because some parts of public spending vary much more sharply with the general economic climate than others. However, the public expenditure White Paper does give the rough outline of total public spending and, in accompanying paragraphs, describes the detailed changes which will tend to push spending on this or that area of activity up or down. Though it suffers the fate of nearly all predictive writing about the economy, that of being proven wrong in the event, it does at least provide a guide to what the Government of the day thinks it is up to and what it intends the future to look like.

The second important indicator each year in the debate on public spending is the annual Rate Support Grant (RSG) for local authorities. This is the amount of money paid out of national tax funds to local authorities to enable them to meet the spending obligations laid on them by national legislation, and which their own income from rents and rates is quite inadequate to cover.

As we have seen, quite a lot of public spending is dictated by law, and quite a lot of that is spent by local authorities, notably on health and education. The town halls and borough treasurers could not afford to meet the cost of schools and hospitals out of local income, and since education and health are essentially national policies, it is not surprising that much of the local cost is met out of national funds. This also helps to smooth out the differences in income levels of different areas of the country, so that taxpayers in the richer parts of the realm subsidize services in poorer regions.

For all these reasons, the government pays RSG to local authorities. With the rise of centrally set policies of public education, public health and other prescribed public services over which town halls have little control, the size of RSG has inevitably grown and now amounts to some 60 per cent of the income of local authorities; their own rates, council house rents and other income account for only 40 per cent.

Because of this development the autumn announcement of the grant looms very large in the public spending calendar. This is not only because the Government will try to curb local authority spending by reducing the grant – and therefore throwing on to authorities which want to spend more the odium of having to increase their rents and rates to meet their spending – but also because it may use the RSG to favour one set of local authorities at the expense of others. Thus, for instance, Conservative Governments are charged with favouring the rural country authorities and penalizing the inner-city areas, while the Labour Party, judged to rely more heavily on urban support at the polls, is charged with doing the reverse.

Over these broad-brush plans for public spending that are announced each year there are fierce debates. The greatest and most hard-fought is perhaps in the Cabinet itself.

Here the whole significance of public spending is crystallized and focused. On the one hand, there is the Government as a whole, trying to balance the national budget so as to prevent too much inflation on the one hand, too much unemployment on the other. The Prime Minister (*any* Prime Minister) and the Treasury Ministers carry that responsibility. On the other hand, there are the spending Ministers with their departmental plans for certain improvements or schemes. There are really two arguments going on.

The first, explained in chapter 1 on the Budget judgement, is about the economic effects of this or that level of public spending. The second is much more like children around a bowl of cherries, each one wanting more than its fair share.

The conduct of this argument is leisurely. Before the end of the summer session of Parliament the Cabinet takes its first cautious look at the next year's plans. From July until about October the wrangle over the bowl of cherries takes place, with the Chancellor of the Exchequer and his lieutenants in the Treasury arguing with the spending Ministers about how much they are to have. In the late autumn there may be one, two or more final Cabinet debates before the White Paper is completed and the public is allowed to know how its money is to be spent – how much will be allocated to agriculture, how much to steel or electricity, housing or roads, defence or schools. And, an important point, how much altogether?

Many economy watchers think that the absolute size of public spending is much more important than the arguments between housing and hospitals, universities or railways.

There are a number of reasons why economists and others worry about the size of the public sector overall. Perhaps the most important is the impression – true or false – that the public services are bureaucratic and inefficient. It is certainly the case (see chapter 6 on wages) that public-sector pay enjoys safeguards which do not seem to operate in the more rough-and-ready free market. And it may be that jobs also are better protected, so that even when times are bad and unemployment is rising sharply, it rises less in the public than in the private sector.

If such factors give cause for concern about efficiency, so does the kind of service that the public sector provides. It is difficult, as mentioned earlier, to assess the 'productivity' of activities like teaching or other social services. In one important sense, it does not matter whether a social services department is efficient in economic terms; what matters is that the elected politicians, local or national, have decided that a certain minimum of support must be given to the elderly or to inner-city renewal. These are political, not economic, judgements.

But taken overall, and alongside such spending as military manoeuvres or diplomatic receptions in foreign parts, they do not provide the 'value added' (see chapter 12) which similar sums of money might produce if spent on other sorts of economic activity. Going further, it is argued that the high level of spending on public services outlined at the start of this chapter actually 'crowds out' other sorts of activity which are more efficient and would, if encouraged, produce a better return in terms of prosperity and employment.

The fundamental argument is that because public services are provided for political reasons, they cannot be as efficient as other services which are provided for the hard economic motive of giving the employer a livelihood. On the other hand, it is strongly argued that the sorts of activities undertaken by the public sector are socially too important to be left to private enterprise. Proponents of public service also insist that the accountability of public servants to town halls or Parliament is essential.

A more down-to-earth cause for concern about the public sector as a whole is that it always loses money. Just as we have seen that local authorities have to call on central tax revenues to meet more than half of their current spending, we also find that total public spending consistently outruns total revenue from all sources – tax, rents, rates and charges.

The problem then arises: how is this over-spending to be met? The answer, though I do not wish to sound frivolous, is the 'National Debt'. Not to put too fine a point on it, successive Governments have borrowed money from wherever they could in order to meet their over-spending.

Every year (with a tiny handful of notable post-war exceptions), government spends more than comes in. Every year, therefore, it borrows. And the borrowing takes the form of selling to the public promises to pay interest on its loans and, eventually, to repay the capital. This borrowing in all its forms, from national savings certificates and premium bonds to British Government stock (gilt-edged), dealt in exclusively on the Stock Exchange in London, grows steadily and forms the National Debt.

In itself, some borrrowing by Governments is inevitable. Just as a family borrows to buy its house or a firm borrows to buy a new piece of equipment or factory, so Governments are expected to borrow for 'capital' investment. A family or a business certainly expects to repay the cost of the borrowing in time, the family within the span of a twenty-five- or thirty-year mortgage, the firm within the life of the equipment purchased, so that when it is worn out the debt incurred to buy it has also been paid off. Governments have no such 'lifetime'. They borrow not just for capital projects like nationalizing the railways or building long-lasting motorways but, in the end, to cover their total expenses, capital and current, which are not met from current income.

This borrowing is called the Public Sector Borrowing Requirement, or PSBR in the jargon of economy watchers. It is published regularly, and the Government sets limits within which it hopes the PSBR will be contained. Within the PSBR is the Central Government Borrowing Requirement, that is, the borrowing by central government Departments. In addition, there is all borrowing by local authorities and the nationalized industries.

The impact of the borrowing requirement on the economy is hotly debated. Concern about it is rather different from that over the size of the whole of public spending. Of course, if public spending were reduced, the borrowing requirement would be reduced also and its influence for bad or good diminished.

The first argument against the Government's running a high borrowing requirement is that it 'crowds out' other borrowers from the sources of funds available. This argument is sometimes taken to absurd lengths, as when on a recent occasion the British and French Governments were examining the possibilities for a Channel tunnel. Both Governments were agreed that public money should not be used, since both wanted to avoid the need to increase their public borrowing for the vast cost of the tunnel. On both sides of the Channel private enterprise was prepared to raise the money and to construct the tunnel. All the private investors sought was a guarantee in case the giant project should founder through government intervention or other crises. For the French Government this posed no problem. A privately financed Channel tunnel, with a government guarantee in the background as a safety net, did not count as 'public' spending so did not fall within the French definition of the PSBR. But on the other side of the Channel the British Treasury ruled that if private money were raised with a government guarantee, then the borrowing was public borrowing and must fall within the net of the PSBR and be deemed to 'crowd out' other things for which the money might have been used.

The paradox of this kind of definition is that identical work

– for instance, the building of pipelines to serve North Sea oil and gas – is deemed damagingly to 'crowd out' other investment plans if undertaken by a public industry or even if guaranteed by the Government, while if it is done by a private enterprise concern, no 'crowding out' is alleged, and the only question is whether the new enterprise will make money or not.

The 'crowding out' argument over public borrowing is the logical extension of the view that public spending simply takes up too much of the economy's resources and efforts. The second area of concern about public borrowing would exist however large or small the public sector were. It turns on the effects of public borrowing on the rate of interest charged for money.

The general view is that the Government has the means, through the Treasury and the Bank of England, to borrow as much as it needs. But even so, the more the Government – and other public borrowers – seek from lenders, the higher will be the rate of interest they will have to pay. This evidently not only has a bad effect on their own finances, pushing up the cost of interest paid as a proportion of all their expenses and therefore making the public sector less efficient with its money as a whole, but it also raises the cost of borrowing for everybody else and, in the view of many economists and more businessmen, puts a very important brake on economic activity and prosperity.

For the first twelve months or so of the 1979 Conservative Government, Ministers insisted on the importance of this relation between public spending, public borrowing and interest rates. But towards the end of 1980 they changed their tune and began to attempt to bring interest rates down before significantly reducing public borrowing. Their reason was that the very high interest rates, if allowed to persist until the lengthy and painful business of reducing public spending and borrowing was complete, would do even more damage to the finances of industry, private and public, than was already being done by the world recession.

At the same time, the Government continued its efforts to reduce public spending and borrowing. As a result, after a set-back in 1981 the Government felt confident enough in 1982 once more to try to reduce interest rates and, with them, the burden of financial costs. This burden, as we shall see in chapter 11, is one of a number of crucial factors in the industrial decisions which, as much as the great decisions of government, affect the climate and success of the economy. Many of these decisions are taken with one eye on the City of London, where confidence in the movement of stock and share prices is monitored daily and where the rate of interest on money is set partly by government influence but by many other factors as well.

The next chapter opens the second section of this book, looking at the corporate decisions which influence affairs and starting at their very heart, the Stock Exchange.

# PART II

# Corporate Decisions

# 9

# The Stock Market

So far most of this book has been about the theory and practice of major economic decisions involving Government, central banks, Ministers and the like. From now on we attempt to descend to the more mundane level of private business. But not all at once. Between the level of government, or international decision-taking, and the personal judgements of individual families and people who are faced with the sort of choices discussed in Part III there is the middle ground of business and industry.

At this level, from the boardrooms of industry to the offices of stockbrokers, and the committee rooms of local government, a great deal of the shape of the economic scene is formed. Making sense of the economy means making sense not just of the big affairs – the Budget, public spending, the National Debt – which have been discussed in the last few chapters but also keeping an eye on what is going on at the next stage down. The Government and its Ministers, not to mention the debates in the House of Commons, may present one view of the economy, but it is by no means the only one; the next stage is to examine the indicators which are not 'official' but which nevertheless tell us a good deal about what is going on.

Probably the most frequently discussed indicator of the nation's financial health is the FT (*Financial Times*) Index, whose every movement, up or down, is charted in the newspapers and which, like the scores during cricket Test Matches, can be dialled on the telephone. Second only to the Dow Jones Index for the New York Stock Exchange, the FT Index mesmerizes savers, investors, businessmen and even politicians and commentators who have nothing to gain or lose by its gyrations.

Almost alone among such indicators, the Dow Jones and FT indices have escaped from the confines of financial journalism and professional analysis into the wider world of pub argument and even literature. Characters in P. G. Wodehouse's novels reminisce about stock market movements, and for most people 'the Wall Street Crash' is instantly understood to mean the cataclysmic autumn day's dealing on the New York Stock Exchange in 1929 rather than a physical collision on that financial highway.

There are any number of reasons for this phenomenon, but two will do to introduce the subject. The first is that in a very rough and ready way the two indicators, the Dow Jones and the FT, can be said to reflect the confidence or lack of it that financial analysts and investors on Wall Street or in the City have in the future economic prospects for all of us. It is easier to look up in the paper what has happened to the stock market than to plough through the complex web of economic indicators, public speeches of Ministers and Opposition leaders to try to find out what is going on and why.

Part of the fascination with Stock Exchange prices, whether the market is 'up' or 'down', is the sense that the insiders who actually deal in the market know something that we do not. At least the Dow Jones Index or the FT gives us a clue to what 'they' are up to.

When I worked in New York in the mid-1960s the genial and efficient teleprinter operator in our tower office building, who sent to London both our articles, news stories and messages and those of any number of people who for one reason or another had access to our teleprinter, suffered a life ruled by the vagaries of the Wall Street market. It was not that he had a fortune invested in the market; he himself stood to gain nothing at all from a good performance by the Dow Jones except a good meal in the evening. Literally, or so he assured us, if the Dow Jones did poorly, his wife would become so nervy and irritable that it was no use expecting a warm welcome and a hot meal when he got home at night. If, by happier chance, the stocks were up and the market was doing well, then he could leave our office after the last message had been sent to London in the confident expectation of a lavish spread and a cheerful spouse. He had a special – if irrational – reason for wanting to know what 'they' were up to, but such absorbed interest in the fact that a handful of people can have such a profound financial and psychological effect is not uncommon. And who are they?

The market is made up of traders and investors. The traders are those who make their living from the activity of buying and selling stocks and shares, government bonds and the myriad other forms of marketable paper which people can and do buy and sell in the various exchanges in the City or the financial districts of other major cities. The commonest practitioner is the stockbroker, who buys and sells shares on behalf of clients, whether private or corporate (like a pension fund, or a trust holding millions of pounds, or a bank). Less well known outside the City itself, are the stock jobbers, or plain 'jobbers', as they are usually known.

This smaller group constitutes the centre of the market. Each firm of jobbers – or member within the firm – actually 'makes the market' in a number of the stocks and shares publicly available. A jobber will always be prepared to buy or to sell the shares in which he trades. Because his books are made up only at fortnightly intervals, he can reckon to balance, for instance, one day's selling of a certain share by another day's buying. He makes his money by always offering shares for sale at a higher price than he would be prepared to pay if the broker turned out to wish to sell. On the London Exchange stockbrokers do not buy or sell from one another, only from the jobbers. When a jobber is approached on the floor of the Stock Exchange by a broker and asked the price of a share, he does not normally know whether the broker is a buyer or a seller, so he quotes two prices, the higher the one at which he will sell, the lower the one at which he will buy. The broker then either discloses his intention to buy or to sell, and a deal is done, or, if he does not like the price, he goes no further. Any jobber soon scents the wind of sentiment among the brokers. If they are all asking him to buy, he knows that they do not want the shares and immediately marks his price down. Equally, if they are all asking him to supply them with shares, he puts his selling price up as far as he dares. That, in its essence, is how those daily or even hourly changes in share prices recorded by the FT Index take place.

The jobbers learn from the brokers – by receiving more 'buy' than 'sell' requests and vice versa – and the brokers make their minds up on the basis of what their clients decide. All of these groups also read the newspapers on their way to work, so a mood is established at the outset; for instance, the jobbers will mark their prices down or up sharply before any business is done, and then the brokers try to take advantage of this.

For the rest of us outside the market the impulses which move share prices sometimes seem mysterious, even suspicious. In late 1982, for instance, share prices were constantly reaching new high levels in London at exactly the same moment that unemployment was climbing steadily through its fourth million and industrial production was at its lowest level for more than fifteen years. Suspicion is also directed at the second class of professionally remote insiders – not the dealers but the investors whose orders to buy or sell drive the market along. For these people the publicly charted movements in the FT Index and so on are important for a second reason, which is much stronger than the general indicator of confidence which the newspapers monitor.

This second reason is that for a great many people professionally engaged in financial management or in business and industry itself the changes in the values of stocks and shares, as measured by the indices, really do matter. This is something well beyond the vague question of confidence, or the lack of it, in the City. This form of concern is the real dollars-and-cents variety, affecting the decisions of the business world, which in turn affect general prosperity, jobs and the output of the whole economy.

In one way the stock markets of the industrial countries,

most especially those of the United States and Britain, genuinely furnish the pivotal forum where all information is to be found and on whose decisions all good and ill in the economy depends. It is not difficult to work out why this might be, why stock markets are genuinely important to far more people than have either a financial or a professional stake in them.

First, there are those who use the stock markets to make money. These people, often working on behalf of others, have at their disposal vast sums. In recent years a growing proportion of the money flowing into the Stock Exchanges has come from institutions rather than individuals. These institutions are enterprises like the great assurance companies, the Prudential and all its competitors, who sell life insurance to individuals all over the country. They invest the proceeds of the premiums in the City of London, so that when the insurance falls due the money will have been earning its keep in stocks and shares. Then there are the pension funds, doing much the same thing, collecting a few pounds a week from millions of workers who will, when their turn comes, be the pensioners benefiting from the funds set aside. These managers also want to do the best they can for their pensioners and so seek the investments which are likely to give the best returns over the years. Competing alongside the pension funds and insurance companies are the merchant banks, investing the money of their clients and advising them of their best opportunities to make profits and to earn income from the stock markets.

And for all of these investors – even down to the individual investing his legacy from an aunt, or a gratuity from the Services, or a lump-sum redundancy payment – there is the army of professional advisers. In the City these are mostly the firms actually engaged in buying and selling stocks and shares for their customers, the stockbrokers and stock jobbers who are the members of the Stock Exchange and whose role we have briefly discussed.

For this fraternity there are two imperatives. They earn their money by the commission charged on buying and selling shares, so that they compete hard for the business of the big clients and of smaller ones. Apart from efficiency and honesty, the most important commodity they have to sell is advice that is accurate and successful. A stockbroking firm is, quite simply, going to get more business and therefore make more money the better the advice it can produce for clients and customers and the more successful its portfolio management. ('Portfolio management' is the term used for the selection and administration of a collection of stocks or shares for an investor by his adviser or stockbroker, the portfolio being, literally, the selection of different shares held at any one moment.)

Disregarding, for the moment, the activities of any individual firm or broker, it is obvious from the foregoing that the City community is extremely greedy for, and full of, the raw information from which good advice and decisions about buying and selling shares can flow. This is part of the fundamental reason why the movement in stocks and shares is important.

Though the motive of the financial community may be to out-perform each other in predicting market movements (and it is possible to make as much money when the market falls as when it rises), the consequence of its activities is to concentrate in one place an enormous amount of information about the detailed performance of the economy. Some of the information may be fairly thin stuff: the City likes a rumour. I remember well much speculation about the Bank of England's policy toward the German mark when the Bank's dealers were spotted buying marks. This, it was thought, heralded some major, but as yet obscure phase of international currency co-operation. The fact was more mundane; it was approaching pay day for the British Army of the Rhine, and the money was needed to pay the troops! But even if some of the information is less than perfect and some of the resulting decisions are bound to be wrong, it is nevertheless the case that an enormous amount of concentrated research into painstakingly collected data about the progress of the economy – nationally, internationally, privately and publicly – informs the daily movements of the stock market.

It is not always easy to read the lessons of these movements, as much depends on many different influences at work at any given moment. It has been said (insultingly, to more than half the world's population) that the market is like a woman; it is impossible to tell why it has behaved in such and such a way or what it will do next. This male chauvinist slur perhaps reveals the very understandable uncertainty about any individual movement in the market. Sometimes motivation is relatively easy to detect: a rise in oil shares may follow an increase in tension in the Middle East (suggesting higher prices); or a general fall in prices if, for instance, American interest rates rise, may suggest either that money will flow away from London to Wall Street or that the pace of the world economy will be slowed down (both bad for business). Often the whole business is unintelligible, as when I, the journalist, telephone a broker or jobber to find out why shares are falling to be told, 'It's the election' — meaning gossip in the Sunday papers about when the next general election will be. This particular form of jitters is really absurd, for if the market dislikes uncertainty – which is the No. 1 truism about it – then the calling of an election will at least get the uncertainty out of the way quickly. What really worries investors at election time is the feeling that any change in Government will upset the present path of economic policy on which their decisions are based, as may even a change in the present Government's majority or strength.

However, over time the market does tend to reflect genuine and well-informed views about the nature of the economy. It has certainly reflected the rather poor performance of the general economy in recent years. In the late summer of 1982, for instance, although the average prices of shares rose to their highest level ever just as unemployment was reaching its post-war peak, the real value of stocks and shares (their purchasing-power value) had fallen back a very long way indeed. The reason was that the rise in share prices and in the dividends paid out on stocks and shares had fallen over the years as the value of money fell faster than the market rose. In this respect, even at the height of the peaks of market values, the worth of stocks and shares declined, just as the vigour of the whole economy had declined in the 1970s.

Within the limits of sudden ebbs and flows of confidence and the uncertain nature of the market's predictive ability, the changes in share prices have tended to reflect the future ever since the great crash of the stock markets of 1929 predicted the world slump which followed. (In that case the actual shock of the fall in share prices itself contributed to the slump: usually a change in share prices does not directly affect subsequent economic trends, except very marginally.)

On the whole, stock market movements tend to predict economic changes with an interval of a year or so. The London market, for instance, was rising strongly when unemployment reached 1 million in 1971–2, but the justification for this rise, which seemed heartless at the time, was the revival in business which followed when the Government, responding to the high unemployment, cut taxes and encouraged economic revival. Similarly, the stock markets of London and New York rose in the autumn of 1982, but not because of any good news then circulating: indeed, the sharpest rises in shares came just as the CBI was being most persistent in its claim that there were no signs of imminent revival in industry. The markets were, as so often, anticipating future events and enjoying the first signs of improving conditions as nominal interest rates were falling on both sides of the Atlantic.

When we come to interest rates, we begin to approach the second way in which stock markets play a crucial role in the economy. For the level of share prices is both set by, and in turn determines, the rate of interest on money; and that factor, the cost of money is one of the vital ingredients in any decision-taking about economic and business policy.

Investment, in the sense of the creation of new equipment for manufacturing, distribution and the like (rather than in the parallel sense of the word of investing stocks and shares), is seen by almost all observers as crucial to the health of the economy. If there is too little investment, industry will age more rapidly, become less efficient and eventually lose out to concerns in which new investment is producing more up-to-date, more economical and cheaper products.

Observers have therefore been particularly worried by the relative lack of interest in the British economy in recent years. Whether from the left, which has argued for more state intervention and the 'direction of investment' by Government, or from the right, which has sought to promote initiative and enterprise, political leaders have held in common that new investment is of the first importance.

From the sidelines those who actually make the investment decisions have tended to discount the efforts of Government to encourage or guide investment. I recall discussing this very point with the then Director General of the CBI at the time when, just before British entry into the EEC, the Prime Minister, Edward Heath, was publicly urging every business and company to invest confidently in anticipation of the golden opportunities ahead.

Was this, I asked, actually happening? Well, the Director General replied, it was certainly CBI policy to encourage investment for new European opportunities, since at that time about 70 per cent of the member firms of the CBI were reporting excess capacity, and unemployment was high. But while most of the individual members thought that investment was a good idea for the nation and for the next chap down the road, they themselves were concentrating on trying to get their existing plants working – and had not got the money or the energy to branch out into new investment.

It was also from the CBI, at the table of the National Economic Development Council (NEDC, or 'Neddy'), that one of the best definitions of the criteria for new investment came. Firms, it was claimed, need three preconditions before investing: (1) the prospect of being able to sell the new products which will flow from the investment; (2) the prospect that those sales will be profitable; and (3) a price for money that is sufficiently low to enable them to go ahead.

By a 'low price for money' businessmen means more than just low interest rates on their bank loans. For a company which has publicly held shares, the higher the price of the shares, the cheaper will be the cost of any money the company raises by issuing more of them (A thousand shares sold to the public at 83p each bring in more money than the same number sold for 78p each, though the dividend paid, which is the cost of money *per share*, may well remain the same.)

Company boards of directors quite simply take the price of their shares into account when deciding whether or not to expand: and it is this that places the stock market at the very centre of investment decisions. This is perhaps the key role of the stock market, as the provider of new money for expansion in industry. It is a role whose importance ebbs and flows with business confidence. A very good measure of economic health is the number of new share issues on the Stock Exchange: in good times the new issues flow in spate; at others they tail away, and high interest rates discourage companies from going to the market to borrow.

The importance of the stock market as a source of funds for investment can be over-stated. Most new investment is not financed from the stock market at all but, as described below in chapter 11, from retained earnings and other sources; yet the market is still at the heart of the process of guarding the value of people's savings and then making those savings, or some of them, available to industry for its modernization and progress.

The market is not without its critics even in this respect. It is pointed out that in countries which have done notably better in investment in their industries, like Germany and Japan, the stock market plays a relatively minor role, and most money for investment comes from the banks, which also hold the savings of the workers in the industries. As a consequence, the very savings of the workers (especially in Japan) are directed straight back into the industries which give them employment, without the mediation of the insurance companies, pension funds and unit trusts or even of the stocks and shares themselves. (In Japan, probably less than 20 per cent of the capital raised by companies is borrowed from the stock market as 'equity'; the rest comes from the banks.)

If there are disadvantages for companies in the British system, they have not been well charted, and the investigation into the City's market by Sir Harold Wilson's reporting team in the early 1980s found that on the whole if companies had worthwhile projects to pursue, they could find the money, one way or another, in the City.

On the other hand, the City's markets provide an unmatched range of investment opportunities for savers and others with spare money in hand. Chapter 17 will look at some of these from the individual's point of view. At this stage suffice it to say that for the industrialist concerned to expand his business or the politician or civil servant trying to order economic policy for the country, the stock market remains one, but just one, of the key factors.

# 10
## Trading Business

In chapter 9 I set out the criteria by which businessmen decide to invest in order to improve their businesses. To recap, they are threefold: (1) the prospect of being able to sell the new products which will flow from the investment; (2) the prospect that those sales will be profitable; and (3) a price for money that is sufficiently low to enable them to go ahead.

To understand how well the economy is faring, it is important to know how businesses are trading – that is, what is happening in the real economy as well as in the financial markets discussed in the previous chapter. For businessmen themselves there is plenty of information under the first two headings mentioned above: the prospect of new sales and the prospect of profit on those sales. And for the onlooker there are plenty of signs too.

Every month the Government issues broad figures for retail trade, so that at least the overall picture is clear. The figures are worth a little attention.

First, they are divided into the different categories of goods that people buy: food and non-food items; 'durables' and 'non-durables' (the former being washing machines, refrigerators, etc., which people buy only occasionally, rather than clothes, shoes, etc., which are more frequently traded). It is not difficult to see how things are going in different sectors of the economy if you keep an eye on these figures, though they do not disclose whether the goods are imported or home-made. We have to look elsewhere for that information.

Then the retail trade figures are divided into value figures and volume figures. Naturally, the value of retail trade rises all the time as prices creep (or rush) upwards, so it is very valuable to have an indication of volume as well. One of the remarkable aspects of the recession of the early 1980s was that while unemployment rose very sharply indeed, and bankruptcies and upsets in industry were rife, and industrial production fell to a point perhaps 15 per cent below its previous peak, the volume of retail sales fell hardly at all. A comparison of these figures gives a graphic and important insight into the nature of the recession: in general, living standards did not fall much (otherwise how could the volume of retail sales have held up so well?), but since manufacturing output and employment both fell, the recession must have bitten in a different way. Indeed it did: the more severe aspect of the recession was not a general fall in living standards but a brisk and painful redistribution of incomes and spending *away* from those who lost their jobs.

Even that abrupt shift was blunted, for many individuals, by redundancy payments which enabled them to continue spending, albeit temporarily. Only when the recession had been running for nearly three years, and the number of people who had been out of work for more than a year reached 1 million, did it become economically significant (as well as socially disastrous), and onlookers began to be worried that a further slow-down would be brought on by the first real drop in consumer spending.

Another point revealed by these retail trade figures in comparison with the output figures is that in spite of the depth of the recession, average incomes were not drastically affected. That is to say, while the impact on an individual family of the recession could be very forceful indeed if one or more income-earning members of the family lost their jobs, the impact on those families in which there were no redundancies and on non-earning groups like pensioners and students was far less.

While it is evident from the figure that there was a shift in real income away from those who lost their jobs (and also from many of the self-employed and small firms whose income is based on sales, not on wages), this redistribution permitted everyone else to carry on much as before. What the retail sales figures show is how narrow was the effect of the recession, how slight overall. This may do more than illustrate the economic pattern of the slump; it may help to explain why the very rapid rise in unemployment did not produce a stronger social or political reaction. Governments are nearly always blamed for bad news on the economic front, but it seems that the criticism directed at the Government of the day, when unemployment rose from 1 to 3 million people, may have been blunted by the fact, revealed in the figures, that living standards were not falling in general and that for many people the recession was something read about in the newspaper but not experienced at first hand.

During the 1980s recession the retail trade figures provided very useful information about what was going on in the ultimate market place, the High Street. But I am reminded that these figures illustrate a trap into which the amateur economist (or even the professional) may fall. Some years ago, when I was writing for the *Daily Telegraph* I found myself, not for the first or last time, at loggerheads with the official interpretation of the figures. 'They' (in this case both the Treasury and the Bank of England) claimed that the figures for April, May and June showed that retail trade was doing well. I, scenting recession, entirely disagreed, thinking that what in fact was happening was a stand-still. These were (by analogy) the figures giving rise to our disagreement: January 100; February 101; March 102.5; April 103; May 103; June 103.

The Treasury, wishing to put the best interpretation on the figures, pointed out during the summer that the rate of retail trade showed growth over the previous period. It was able to pursue this line even to the point of including the June figure, for evidently the average level of trade April–June was (at 103), better than the average January–March level (at less than 102). My jaundiced eye, however, settled on the fact that there had been no growth whatever in the three months April–June and that, however you looked at the figures, it was quite wrong to claim that even the trend of sales was still rising when for those three months the index had stood at the same point. I do not believe that the argument was ever exactly resolved: I retained my position, but no doubt when a dull autumn succeeded a stagnant summer the official observers continued to maintain that their analysis had been fully justified at the time.

This cautionary note illustrates one point only about the interpretation of official figures. There are some figures, like those for retail trade, which can yield useful information about the economy quarter by quarter, even month by month. Others, like the index of average earnings, tell us very little except on the basis of annual comparison. The reason for this is, broadly, that people only get one pay rise a year, and not all at the same time of year, so the sensible statistician likes to take in a whole year (thus including almost everyone's pay rise) rather than the monthly or quarterly changes in the index, which cover only a fraction of the total.

To return from the niceties of statistical interpretation to what the observer of the economy should look out for when assessing the general state of business trading, there are a number of other useful guides. Working, as it were, up the scale from the High Street to the factory itself, the next guide to prosperity is the figure for car sales, registrations and production.

It is difficult to envisage Britain – indeed, the whole industrial world – without cars. As the great assemblers, the Fords, Renaults, Toyotas, vie with one another and between them provide a mass of work not only for their own employees but also for many more people who are indirectly employed in component factories, the oil industry and even road building, the importance of the motor industry needs no emphasis.

Here the essential figures are sales, output and imports. The new registration figures show the overall picture of car sales but do not indicate where the cars have come from. For that the observer must turn to the industry's own figures, supplied by the Society of Motor Manufacturers and Traders, which do provide a break-down of sales by manufacturer. Take the two together and, at least as far as motoring is concerned, it is possible to argue both the general prosperity and the relative success of foreign cars versus home-produced ones, BL versus the rest and so on.

Moving on from the motor, the next important indicator of general prosperity is the rate of sales in the housing market and also the amount of new house building going on. Housing is divided into several markets: new and second-hand, public and private. Official figures chart housing in several ways: for each sector (public and private) both housing 'starts' and housing 'completions' are published monthly, and together these figures provide an accurate picture of the supply of new housing. There are also figures for new house orders placed.

So much for new housing: these figures give guides to both the general state of the economy and the relative performance of the public and private sectors. They are complemented by other figures, more revealing of the general state of the housing market, from the building societies. What the building society figures show is the total turnover in the private sector of both new and second-hand housing sales. As private housing is a very large component in total housing, building society figures give a more general picture of the trade in housing, especially since a large proportion of houses bought and sold are second-hand and do not therefore make any impact on the building figures for new homes.

With total spending on housing running at about twice the level of spending on new buildings, the second-hand trade is evidently significant. It is noteworthy, for example, that the decline in the housing industry in total between 1979 and 1982 was much steeper in the public sector than in the private, so that while council house building declined by nearly 50 per cent, the fall in the private sector was less than 33.3 per cent. And building society loans, though faltering, continued at roughly the same level throughout the period. The squeeze therefore could be seen to affect public housing most markedly, while even in the very trough of recession mortgages were still being sought, and found, at much the same level as in recent years.

If retail trade, the motor business and the housing industry give a fairly complete picture of the state of the economy from the consumer's and the family's point of view, that is by no means the end of the story. The next patient needing analysis is commerce itself. Here there are a handful of particularly important series which let us know what is going on. To start with, there are the figures for profits. In both the private sector, where profit is necessary if any business is to be done, and the public sector, where lack of profit means that the taxpayer has to find the money (thus injecting a measure of social activity into the proceedings), figures for profits are among the most important indicators of health and future prospects. The word 'profit' is sometimes misleading, however, as was demonstrated by a public opinion poll some years ago which elicited from more than half of those polled the statement: 'Profits go directly into the bosses' pockets.' This showed clearly that the people who had been approached had no idea that all but the distributed profit, or dividend, is retained in a business, and that even the dividend goes to all the shareholders, including insurance companies, pension funds and so on (discussed in chapter 9), and not 'into the bosses' pockets'. That naive misunderstanding of the cash flow of industry is not the only confusion about profits. And if you are one of those who still think profits go straight into bosses' pockets, see below in chapter 12 and look out for the concept of 'value added' discussed there. But even without going into that refinement, there is always a lot to say about profits and how they are faring.

At the time of writing the best method of measuring profit is the subject of heated debate among the very professionals who are charged with the measurements, the accountants. Their problem 'inflation accounting', will be discussed in the next chapter, but here the main point is that cash profits should also be measured by what they can buy. At times of high inflation the figures for profits, like the figures for much else, may be distorted by rapid changes in prices, and the best way to get a feel for 'true' profit is to find profits based on current costs, not on the historic costs of the business. (though, as will be seen later, there are two sides to this argument as well!)

Beyond the figures for profits, which companies publish in general only once or twice a year (although one or two honourable exceptions produce quarterly estimates), the more frequently disclosed barometers of industrial health are the simpler figures for industrial output, stocks and sales. These figures, once they have been adjusted for changes in efficiency like automation and for other devices designed to increase productivity (discussed in the next chapter), bring the student of economic health, by way of the sales and production side of the coin, close to the heart of the matter – the general level of economic activity.

Apart from GNP, or industrial production, the most common yardstick that is used to gauge the general prosperity and success of the economy is, of course, unemployment. Whatever else is happening, persistent unemployment suggests a failure to run the economy at its full potential. (Incidentally, countries differ vastly over what that full potential should be: on the Continent a far lower proportion of the total population is expected to be in the working population than in Britain; the 'full employment' from which the country has recently fallen so far short is actually set at a level considerably higher than in Europe.)

That being said, the debate rages most keenly over the means by which to achieve full or high employment. In spite of the profound differences between the theories of the pure market economy, the mixed economy with plenty of state interference and the concept of pure socialism, there is agreement that investment by industry – whether state- or privately owned – is crucial. If people are to be productively employed (always remembering that there is someone else breathing down your neck for the business), they must have the tools for the job. That means that vast sums of money must be deployed to pay for the machinery, the infrastructure and the factories themselves which go to make up the whole industrial and commercial apparatus on which the rest of the economy depends.

# 11

## Industrial Investment

One theme which has run through much of this book so far is the importance of investment in industry. It is also one of the preoccupations of politicians, trade unionists and, of course, businessmen. Previous chapters have glanced at the three criteria deemed necessary before investment decisions are made; they can be rephrased thus: market, margin and money.

No one except a philanthropist, a romantic or a military commander is going to spend money to produce goods or services that nobody wants or will pay for. So, from the humblest one-man business to the giant multi-national, the market comes first.

Sometimes this fact is disguised. A craft workshop or village pottery may be set up because those working in it seek a particular kind of life – an escape from urban sophistication, perhaps, or the 'good life'. But in order to make a success of even so modest an 'investment', something must be produced which can be sold or bartered to keep the concern going.

Markets are strange creatures. They range from commodity markets in staple goods (cotton, wheat, or coffee and tea, or copper, zinc, silver and tin), which seem permanent and immutable, to fleeting and fashionable markets in goods like skate-boards, or space invaders, or CB radio. Some, of course, are a mixture. Denis Healey, as Labour Chancellor of the Exchequer, got tremendous stick when, in setting the rate of VAT, he put household refrigerators in the upper or 'luxury' band. Where had he been for the past thirty years people demanded; how did he keep his milk fresh? Clearly, the refrigerator started as a luxury, even a novelty, but had become by the 1970s as routine an item of household supply as a cooker or even (stretching it a bit) a bed to sleep in.

Markets are not entirely objective. It is often possible for businessmen to shift them, and while we are still in the kitchen, here is a cautionary tale from the 1950s. After the Second World War it became clear to some manufacturers that the next fashion – or at least a trend well worth following – was going to be fitted kitchens. Nothing very grand, but the cupboard under the sink and nice flush worktops. History does not disclose who the inspired marketing man was who got the industry together and suggested that they should all agree to sell nothing for ten years but white fitted kitchens. But they did, and then, after a decade, they all moved on together to sell coloured kitchens, not to mention mock pine, eye-level grills and the rest of the paraphernalia. In that case the marketing strategy also demanded investment, which is where the decision-making process comes in.

A more dramatic case of a similar sort was the introduction of long-playing records. The investment there had to be very large: for if everyone was going to make money out of the new microgroove, slowed-down discs, then they would all have to be prepared together. In that case the market followed the investment, which itself followed the boffins' inventiveness. These enormous investments in complete new technologies, producing entirely new products, are not all that rare. In one lifetime there has been the whole of aviation, rocketry, radio, television and most of motoring. What, it may be asked, did people do in the nineteenth century? What will they be doing in the twenty-first?

When I worked briefly in a giant multi-national company that traded in rubber we used to ponder about the company's future. The tyre business was going through a particularly bad time – tyres being among the major products (no, the dominant one, and for good reasons) that actually *cost* money to make and sell in Europe. One could reflect that eighty years before the company had not made any car tyres at all but was already established in twenty countries around the world, and if the energy buffs were right, the odds seemed to be that in eighty years' time we should not be making many, if any, tyres. But how, we asked ourselves, to get from here to there? How to adapt to new ideas, new technologies and, most of all, how to tell now what the new market will be then?

Markets can lead, as they usually do; they can also be led or influenced by inventors, entrepreneurs, politicians and the like. (There is no 'market', properly speaking, for armaments except that created and maintained by political forces manifested through political leaders. It is the genius of social organization that has created this multi-billion-pound worldwide industry to replace the bow and arrow, the shotgun or even the six-gun for self-defence.) However, most investment decisions taken in industry are influenced by less profound considerations than that. Mostly, it is back to the basics, which is where margin comes in as well as market.

Standard economic theory tells us that in a perfect market supply will equal demand at a certain price (called the 'equilibrium' price) and that the prevailing price in any market influences demanders' and suppliers' decisions about whether or not to buy. A rise in price of a good, for example, may discourage buyers, so demand will be reduced; then some of the people who produce the good may be forced to cut back their supply in the face of an impending surplus.

This is what happened in the tyre industry in Europe in the 1970s. All over Europe in the late 1960s the tyre business had looked very good. Demand for motoring, and therefore for tyres, was on the up and up, and so the multinational tyre companies all made investments in new plants to produce more tyres. They were also destined to produce more than simply a greater volume of tyres, however, because, following the success of Michelin with its 'X' radial tyre, when the French firm's monopoly of the new design came to an end everyone else had to start making the radial tyres, which would run, effectively, about twice as far as its predecessor, the cross-ply tyre.

Then came the oil crisis of 1973–4. While motoring by no means ceased, it did stop growing. So the companies which had made large new investments in a growing market found, within a space of about five years, that they had twice as much product and barely 10 per cent more sales. Suddenly the industry in Europe was over-suplied with capacity by a staggering 40 per cent, and there followed a ghastly couple of years while each of the giants hung on, hoping the others would bite the bullet and shut down a factory or so to reduce the surplus. Eventually, and perhaps too late, they nearly all had to close down factories and reduce supplies.

But what, in the meantime, of the economists' equilibrium between supply, demand and price? Although imperfectly, the laws of market economics were working. While the prices of many other goods were steadily rising and the labels on tyres also showed higher prices in the late 1970s than ten years earlier, the real price of the products had fallen dramatically. There was, of course, the fact that a new tyre now ran perhaps twice as far as the same commodity ten years ealier; then there was the general fall in the value of money. Take the two together, and what the motorist was paying per mile – which is, of course, what he is buying when he pays for a new tyre – was down by a staggering 40 per cent in real terms. No wonder the industry was in trouble. In this case, because of the weakness of demand and the important of competing in new technological standards, almost the whole benefit of the radial tyre breakthrough had been passed on to the customer, almost none of it retained in the industry. What had happened had made those new investments back in the 1960s look sick. And why? Not because the market collapsed (it did not – it only grew more slowly), but because the second ingredient, margin, simply was not there any more.

If a guru had told all the European tyre makers that within ten years the products of their new investment would be selling at a loss, or close to it, they would never have invested on such a scale. In this particular case what followed was a painful scramble out from under the consequences of investment decisions which, with hindsight, could be seen to have been made at just the wrong moment. It is a story which could be repeated in a large number of other industries: steel, ship building and, perhaps most well-known, man-made fibres, a comparatively young industry littered with the ruins of over-investment.

My friend James Morrell, economic forecaster and guru in his own way, liked once to tease orthodox economic and industrial commentators by advancing the theory that in Britain we had invested not too little (as was the conventional wisdom) but too much, so that every unit of output, every hour of work, was over-burdened with the cost of paying for much too much past spending on machinery, equipment and so on. On the face of it, expensive investment does require that vital ingredient, margin, or profit to pay for it: and the second of our two prerequisites, profit on the product of new investment that is sufficient to pay for the investment itself and leave something over for the future of the business and for the shareholders, state or private, is probably the most important of all.

Of course, one element of the cost of the investment that its produce must cover is the cost of the money itself. The third of the three prerequisites for investment may be the least important, but it is still a prerequisite, not just an option! By far the largest proportion of money for investment comes, in fact, from the earnings of the business itself. In every company's accounting a certain amount of income is set aside every year for the replacement of equipment; indeed, companies are granted tax relief for depreciation. The cost of such money is low: in fact, it should properly be measured by reference to the sum that the money could otherwise have earned if it had been lent out at interest. The manager of any business has, naturally, to decide on what to spend its income: to choose between new investment and other forms of spending. In trying to make the decision, he will want the nearest thing to an impartial, objective measure of return on the money. The phrase 'opportunity cost' has been used elsewhere to describe the manager's arithmetic, and it expresses neatly the heart of the question, implicitly looking the manager in the eye and asking whether

the cost of any investment, compared with any other opportunity foregone, is worth it.

But even if the financial sense of an investment meets the
tests set out above, market, margin and money, there remains
one further, and extremely difficult question. This is the matter
of 'inflation accounting'. Arguments still swirl about the un-
answerable question of how to value the various components
of an industrial or commerical concern. At the core of this
matter is the issue of whether the value of the capital plant of
any company or firm should be measured by what it cost to
install or by what it would cost to replace. It is, writ large, the
householders' dilemma about how much insurance is needed
to cover the knick-knacks and furniture in the house: accumulated over the years or left to you in the wills of relations, they
do not seem to have 'cost' much, but once stolen, broken or in
need of replacement, these inconsiderable trifles turn out to be
worth a great deal of money. And the same is true, finally, of
the essential plant and equipment on which industry runs: the
lathes, the overhead cranes for moving work from one end of
the shop to another, the girders, roof, air-conditioning system
of the fabrication department, the typewriters of the clerical
department, the fabric of daily life and work – endlessly need
replacement.

Depreciation is the way in which enterprises allow for the
replacement of these vital sinews of their business. So much is
set aside each year to renew existing machines and the like.
But the problem is that often the amount set aside is a fraction
of the cost of the original installation (say: this item cost
£20,000 and will last twenty years, so let us set aside £1,000 a
year for it). But then when the new machine is wanted its cost is
not £20,000 but £150,000 or what have you, and where's the
money to come from? If, instead of setting aside £1,000 a year
for twenty years the accountants had set aside £7,500 a year,
they might have had enough money to pay for the new machine
– but where would the profit have gone in the meantime? If
even in times of 7 or 8 per cent annual inflation enough money
is set aside to replace at the true cost the equipment used in

industry and commerce, the whole calculation of profit and loss is transformed.

The paradox is that at a time when money is losing value – that is, at a time of rapid 'inflation' – it is argued that the sensible thing to do is to invest in capital goods, be they houses, or machinery to make things, or land. But for industry such investment is relatively short-term. The factory and its equipment will wear out, and one factor which has tended in recent years to reduce the pace of replacement, and therefore the average efficiency of plant and equipment, is the very fact, referred to above, that the true cost is far higher than the 'historic cost' at which the machine or building was bought in the first place.

Although investment is supposed to be the best 'hedge' against inflation protecting the investor against a fall in the value of money, the very fall in money values postpones, and often prevents, the vital decisions that industry and commerce should take to make productive investment. One of the factors inhibiting investment at times like these is, in effect, uncertainty. Inflation contributes to uncertainty, and a return to slower inflation not only enables the accountant to do his sums on surer ground but also gives the managers who made the decisions a firmer basis on which to judge opportunities and therefore to make investment decisions. Inflation is not the most important, but neither is it by any means the least, of the impediments to practical investment.

# 12

# Company Decisions

In chapter 11 I looked at industrial investment, the factors which govern the decisions of companies about whether to invest or not and the importance these have for the economy as a whole. But while industrial investment is a key guide to the future health of the economy, it is by no means the only aspect of business life on which decisions have to be made constantly by company managers and directors.

To a very great extent, the whole economy is driven by the effectiveness or otherwise of the private sector of business, industry and commerce. Take away the activities of thousands of individual firms, companies and partnerships and what is left? Just the political and service structures of the country – by all means, the schools, hospitals and universities, agriculture (though without much machinery!) and the churches, Parliament and local government. But without the success of industry, the wages that it pays and the taxes on those wages, how would these things be paid for?

So the economist must be interested in the commercial affairs of the country and the sorts of decisions taken both in the boardrooms and closer to the shopfloors of industry and commerce. Many of these decisions fall into four main areas – design, manufacture, marketing and industrial relations (or personnel) – and within each are many subdivisions. For instance, included in design are many decisions about function, durability, visual appeal and, of course, the nature of the product itself. In manufacture are included decisions about, for instance, the degree of mechanization of the factory, shift working, product testing, safety and how much to attempt in one concern as opposed to buying in from suppliers special skills or bulk deliveries at lower cost.

Marketing comprehends a great range of decisions; identifying a market for a new or modified product, test marketing, selling (direct, by mail, through wholesalers, distributors or retailers) and, of course, advertising (how much, and on TV or in newspapers?). Just as important, back at the factory, decision taking embraces industrial relations, including employee communication, consultation, trade unions relations (closed shop or recognition at all?) and terms of employment, ranging from canteens to retirement pensions. It is not, therefore, as simple as just deciding on a product to make, agreeing its price and then getting on with it. Nor is settling pay always simple.

In one concern with factories across the country that needed similar employees, from unskilled labourers, to semi-skilled tool-setters and the like up to skilled staff, there were national negotiations with the trade unions recognized in the industry. While the national agreement could be said to be fair and gave the overall company a strong negotiating position as well as being welcome to the unions, for managers the pay levels meant that in relatively well-off areas (the East Midlands, the south) they were struggling to hold on to workers who could find jobs just down the road paying a few pounds more, while in poorer areas (South Wales, Merseyside) men getting the same money were the envy of their neighbours and relatively hard to persuade to accept innovation or even overtime working.

Decision-taking in industry is, then, an extraordinarily complex business, which has far-reaching consequences outside the concern or factory involved. There is a vast literature of business management; many training schools and institutes have been set up to train managers and directors; and the business associations that bring together managers of all sorts are legion. One of the things that makes decision-taking in industry so demanding is simply that no two sets of circumstances are precisely alike. Into most decisions intrudes an element of 'feel' for the situation, which is why managers, sometimes confounding theorists, set more store by experience than by high, but youthful, qualifications.

However, managers neccessarily inhabit the same world as the rest of us, read the same newspapers, hear the same politicians, and experience inflation, depression or prosperity in much the same way. It ought to be possible to isolate at least some of the things which make for good or bad management, which divide the sheep from the goats in management terms.

The conventional wisdom about management decision-making makes much of experience, concentration, specialization, 'man management' and the indescribable 'flair'. A good manager will also be thoroughly trained and a good communicator but may come from almost any side of the business. He may be an accountant or a salesman, an engineer or a skilled worker promoted through the system. Everyone agrees that the best managers are, without exception, hard workers.

But these virtues, and their opposites, are so general as to be almost meaningless, and in looking further to find what makes good or bad management decisions I think it worth focusing on two broad areas.

First, there is the question which all good managers should have decided before they address a problem: 'What is business *for*?'

Very few firms or companies exist solely to make money for their owners: equally, few exist solely to provide jobs for their employees, It is possible to envisage, for instance, a small family bank on a partnership basis which comes close to the former end of the spectrum, simply the making of money, and to recall co-operative ventures, like the John Lewis Partnership, which do very well indeed at the latter end, their main philosophy being partnership among all the workers in the concern. But even for these two extreme cases, and for all others, there is another essential without which neither aspiration could be met, and that is the need to satisfy the customer. It would be as great an over-simplification to say that they all existed only to satisfy their customers, as it would be to ignore the customer altogether.

In every management decision, then, there must be the element of aiming to detect which of the parties to the enterprise most need to be satisfied at the outcome: the owners, the customers or the work force. A clear perception of what the business is about may help the manager to decide sensibly and to get it right more often than not. On the other hand, it is possible to have a clear perception of what business is for and still get it wrong.

The most famous failure of the last decade or so was perhaps the collapse of Rolls-Royce Ltd in February 1971. It would not be an exaggeration to say that the senior managers of Rolls-Royce knew exactly what Rolls-Royce was *for* – it was for excellence, invention and being the best. You might, without cruelty, say that they believed in their own history, their own brand image. The crash was caused, among other things, by the enormous cost of developing the best jet engine in the world for airliners, the RB-211, and employing in this development an entirely new material for jet engines, a carbon-fibre compound, at a time when sales of new engines were very hard to come by.

In the wake of the crash many stories circulated about how Rolls-Royce had been mismanaged. This one may be apocryphal but, true or false, it points a moral. It is said that a year or so before the final collapse the old government-sponsored Industrial Reorganization Corporation (IRC) was in touch with Rolls-Royce about putting public money into the RB-211 engine project. An emissary from the IRC – which was a financially tough-minded outfit, albeit set up by a Labour Government to nudge industry into shape – arrived at the Rolls-Royce headquarters in Derby. He would like, he said, to meet the finance director of Rolls-Royce. (To those new to this sort of fable of business adventure I should explain that the finance director in any company is the member of the board who is responsible for sanctioning the spending of the company's money. He is the 'no'-man, whose opposition the engineers, the marketing men, the personnel managers must overcome if they are to spend money on any new project, from a new coat of paint on the factory to opening a branch office in Singapore. The finance director, often a chartered accountant is, in short, the keeper of the company's books.)

Picture then, the pin-striped, briefcase-bearing accountant, arriving from the IRC headquarters in London, to be greeted by the most senior executive of Rolls-Royce Ltd. In his bag he has money (or the offer of it), but he wants to see what shape Rolls-Royce is in before comitting himself or it. He would like, he said, to see the finance director. 'The who?' replied Rolls-Royce.

Exaggerated, perhaps, but there is no doubt that the Rolls-Royce of those years was a company in which control of finances took second place to engineering innovation. Rolls-Royce knew what it was 'for' but neglected good housekeeping. If the board had been more keenly aware of the second insight into business which is looming larger and larger for the good manager, it might have avoided catastrophe. This second yard-stick, on which the shrewd eye will be pinned, is the concept of 'added value'.

Companies, their customers and their employees and management are always worrying about money. The customers think the prices are too high: the management fears the cash-flow is too low and worries about profits and margins; the workforce naturally worries about pay and may think that management, the owners, shareholders or whoever are doing too well out of the business.

These worries sometimes muddy the waters of decision-taking, especially at the factory. As I was reminded in chapter 10, people have some odd ideas about profits, including a high proportion which supposes that profits go straight into the bosses' pockets. The accountancy convention that profit is all the money coming into the business through sales *minus* operating expenses, purchase of materials and wages tells only a small part of the story. It focuses attention on profit, which may be only a very small part of the total affairs of the company. To get away from this conventional view of company health, a number of professionals and businessmen now focus on the added value concept.

The added value produced in any company can be very easily worked out: it is the value of the total sales of the company *minus* the cost of goods and services bought in from outside. Everything else is added value. What then happens is that this sum, far larger than conventionally assessed profit, is divided up. By far the largest component of added value is the wages and salaries of the staff and works. The next item is the cost of money used in the business and the amount of tax paid by the business. Both of these are paid to 'outsiders'. The first, the cost of money, is essential to the business simply to provide the factory, the equipment and so on – the 'capital' of the business. And tax, well, we all have to pay tax. Finally, there is the money left over, which will be divided between keeping the business going and adding to the reserves or investments of the business.

The last items are important. The added value left over for the business, and either used or earmarked for use in maintaining the business, is 'depreciation': without it the equipment and capital of the business would just wither away. It is only after setting aside the funds to pay for this aspect of the business that the last residue can be added to the reserves of the business, be it in bank balance or investments. And, of course, in poor trading conditions, after dividing up the added value in the way described above the last figure may be a minus number, and then the reserves of the concern actually shrink or its borrowings increase.

The concept of profit is important, not least because, as described in chapter 9, companies can raise new money on the Stock Exchange with an ease, and at a price, which is directly related to their profits. And since most major businesses in the private sector are public companies, whose shares are quoted on the Stock Exchange and which have issued thousands of shares to shareholders who legally 'own' them, they obviously have a duty to make sure that the profit is there to provide the money to pay the dividends to the shareholders or owners who put up the money in the first place.

But it may be that the effort to maximize profits may obscure for managers other aspects of the running of a concern which are not to do with raising money or rewarding the shareholders. On scrutinizing a manufacturing business through the lens of added value it becomes immediately apparent that the relative importance of the parties to the enterprise is reversed. The most important are the customers, who provide the gross receipts. Next in importance may well be the suppliers of materials and energy, which have to be wrought into the final product. But in this process of adding value by far the most important beneficiaries of the existence of the enterprise are the employees. They contribute the greatest fraction of value added and take away the greatest fraction of the resultant cash flow. Management, shareholders, even the bankers, are nowhere in this race.

Any manager who does not understand this aspect of the running of a business is likely to fall into an error that is the opposite of the one which entrapped Rolls-Royce. That company, it seems, dwelt too little on its growing financial problems, but the entirely profit-oriented manager may run into shallows of a different sort if he neglects the wider nature of the business. And one thing is certain: however the figures for a business are analysed, if the added value is not enough, the business will eventually fail.

However, even a manager who is a paragon of financial rectitude and is aware of the importance of added value as well as of profit may run into a further, and perhaps besetting, difficulty in industry. Industrial relations are extraordinarily difficult to handle with complete success. The history of the labour movement and the growth of the 'them-and-us' division in society and especially in industry is entirely outside the scope of this book. But that doesn't mean that the student of decision-taking in business, industry and commerce, private or public, can get away from the present state of affairs. It seems to me that there are three aspects of industrial relations which are general enough in scope to warrant comment.

The first is the way in which in many industries management has largely conceded the matter of communication to the trade unions. A great deal of argument is on parade about the need for good communications within industry, from management to the shop floor, but examples like the occasion on which a message of the first importance to all employees (in fact, a copy of a letter to them all) was banned from the company notice-boards, on the grounds that it would in some way be 'bypassing' trade union channels, are far from uncommon. It will be an uphill battle to recover from this loss of the very means of communication and to regain a state of affairs in which workers are brought into touch with managers directly, as both trade union and management theory desire.

The second aspect of industrial relations which should be in the minds of industrial decision-makers is the evolution, now virtually complete, of the professional trade unionist. The full-time trade union official, at plant, local, regional or national level, has a special and distinctive role in industrial relations. He is required to earn his living by trade union activity. Much of this can loosely be labelled 'welfare' work on behalf of those members of the union who need help. And any trade union official knows that in this aspect of his work he will be un-popular with management, if only because most of the personal cases with which he has to deal are those of workers who have, for some reason, fallen short of what is expected of, or by, them. The employee who is working satisfactorily, and is satisfied, does not trouble the union official or, through him, management.

But beyond the welfare work of dealing with problems and cases, the professional trade unionist will also sometimes wish for wider fields in which to operate. It is here that strains arise which take up a great deal of management decision time and effort and can radically alter the course of the business. For one thing, the professional trade unionist may bring general prin-ciples of industrial relations practice to bear in a way which amounts almost to disingenuousness. I have myself heard the cry of 'No consultation' go up from senior national trade union officials when redundancies were announced when, only a month or so before, I had spent all day at a serious, analytical and entirely frank conference between senior management and the very same unionists.

There could be no question whatever that all the trade union leaders had as clear a picture of the trouble besetting their industry as did all the managers. And at the place of work the employees, down to shop-floor level, had known for more than *three years* that the plant's continued existence hung by the twin threads of higher productivity and orders won in a market which was shrinking and over-supplied. In short, everyone knew, with an awful inevitability, what was likely to happen. And when it did happen the trade union officials protested most vigorously. They were, in a sense, doing what they were there to do, earning their living. But it is an inescapable aspect of industrial relations that the same people had recognized the state of play at the earlier conference. Perhaps that frank recognition had come partly because that conference had been held behind closed doors, with no press, no reporting, no publication of anything that was said which tended to show trade unionists acknowledging market problems.

It may be that the national stance of the professional trade union official is a reflection of very simple grass-roots or shop-floor attitudes and positions. Take a hypothetical case. Among any group of workers on the shop floor, in any industrial concern, there are likely to be those who have some little extra energy, some added ambition, which naturally prompts them to out-perform their colleagues. Continuing with this hypothesis, take a couple of such men and let them find alternative avenues for their extra talents and energies. One, let us say, enters trade union activity, becomes in due course a shop steward; the other concentrates his extra effort at the work bench, catches the foreman's eye and progresses up that ladder towards supervisor, foreman, junior management. The point of this hypothesis is that these two are among the most able of their peers. It is precisely their talents which have led to their new, extra responsibilities. Then examine the roles that they are playing.

The supervisor or foreman might fairly be described as the 'customer's man' on the shop floor. His job is to make sure that the batches of work get through on time, with few rejects and the minimum of complaints. Though his line responsibility may be to the next senior manager, in practice it is the customer who benefits from the quality of work he supervises. For the shop-steward the extra responsibilities that he has assumed are quite different. His concern must be the terms and conditions of his workmates. Though both he and the supervisor are interested in the continued existence of the business and its success, in the day-to-day work of the plant their interests will often be at odds. He will want longer tea breaks, the foreman shorter ones. These two men – who got where they are by being the most able among their group – may well end up pulling not in the same direction but on different ends of the same rope.

Finally, to arrive at the end of this long hypothesis, the point to be grasped is that there are no 'goodies' and 'baddies' in all this. In contemporary British industry shop steward and foreman both incontrovertibly represent legitimate interests. Anyone who is trying to understand the labyrinthine nature of decision-taking in British industry must understand that. And those decisions are of daunting complexity. No wonder, as I read in a recent press notice from the CBI, the director general of that august body suggests there should be a Queen's Award for personnel management, to go alongside those for exporting and invention!

The legitimate aspirations of trade unionists exist not just at shop-floor level but all the way to the top. At the start of the 1979 Conservative administration Ministers laid much stress on the relationship between high money wage settlements and subsequent unemployment. At that time I discussed the theory of 'pricing workers out of jobs', as it was characterized, with a number of trade unionists, and not one but two general secretaries of large, public-sector unions told me firmly that the role of elected trade union leaders was not to take into account macroeconomic theories of unemployment but to go to the table and negotiate the highest possible cash awards for their members. And, of course, this was a genuine position; it is not undermined by the acceptance by work forces like British Leyland or the National Coal Board at ballots or meetings of offers lower than those sought by their negotiators and endorsed by their trade union leaders. The legitimacy of the elected leader remains, but his judgement of what his members want to do is at fault. Michael Edwardes at British Leyland frequently read the temper of the work force better than did the trade union leadership, and Joe Gormley, from the trade union side, showed an equally reliable insight into what mineworkers wanted: action in 1972 and 1974 but not in 1981 or 1982.

There is no field in management decision-taking more pored over than industrial relations, but it is worth ending this brief survey of some of the factors involved with the observation that a great many of the decisions which are taken, and of the agreements which are reached, are good ones. The late Lord Feather, when General Secretary of the TUC, once parried a press question about the 'high level' of strikes in British industry. He said that for 97 per cent of the time in British industry work proceeded normally, without interruption, and he added, 'When your son comes home from school with 97 per cent in his exams, you don't clout the lad.'

# 13

## International Trade

More than one quarter of all commerce and business done in Britain is done with foreigners – importing or exporting, buying or selling goods or services across the borders of the country. And every day there is a massive movement of cash across the frontiers to settle bills for trade and also for foreign investment. Britain may be an island (or rather islands), but her trade with the rest of the world is extremely important, as, for reasons which will emerge, is the way in which foreign economies manage their affairs.

Until a very few years ago, the monthly trade figures used to rouse the financial and political communities to a frenzy of excitement, either pleasurable or the reverse, and were seen as a key barometer of the health of the country. They were taken as a guide to whether Britain was paying her way in the world; and if the figures were bad for long, we had a 'balance of payments crisis'.

By and large, the discovery and exploitation of North Sea oil has (probably temporarily) set the impact of trade to one side. The country is enjoying a period of relative comfort in international trade, and while some experts are worried about the loss of markets which may be taking place behind the skirts of a comfortable balance of payments position (see below), there is no longer that sense of mini-crisis which used to attend bad sets of trade figures in the past.

There is another important reason why the trade figures do not matter as much as they used to. Britain now has much more money on hand to pay the foreign bills which pile up when the trade figures are bad and imports come in faster than exports go out.

An important measure of a trading nation's health is the state of the reserves, or official reserves, as they are sometimes called. The reserves are the sums held in foreign currencies and gold by the authorities – in this case the Bank of England – which rise and fall according to the flow of money into and out of the country. For example, the value of the official reserves in February 1982 at more than £10,000 million, would have bought two and a half months' worth of imports if all foreign earnings had stopped dead. This may seem a small margin, but it is a great deal more comfortable to work with than the much narrower margin of between one month and six weeks which was often the value of the reserves in the days of balance of payments crises before the coming of the oil.

Another key change has taken place since the early 1970s which makes the monthly trade figures less important in the eyes of the government and the financial community. This is the fundamental change in the relation between sterling and the currencies of the rest of the world. From the end of the Second World War until 1971 the nations of the non-Communist world operated an agreed system of fixed but movable exchange rates between their currencies. For instance, the rates between the two most important, the dollar and the pound sterling, were from 1949 to 1967 $2.80 per £1; then, following the British devaluation of 1967, $2.40 per £1; then briefly, after the dollar devaluation of 1971, £2.60 per £1. Following the collapse of the fixed exchange rate system in 1971–2 (the pound was officially 'floated' free of the dollar and the rest in the summer of 1972), the exchange rate for the pound against the dollar has fallen as low as $1.45 and has risen to more than $2.00 on occasion.

This chapter started by looking at the trade figures and claimed that they do not have the gripping importance now that they used to have. This is partly because of the new exchange rate system, which allows currencies to 'float' freely up and down, as they have been doing since 1971. This point perhaps needs a mechanical explanation, which may help to show how trade, the reserves and currency values are linked and, even more important, what effects their movements have on the general economy.

First, the balance of payments. This is composed of all the transactions across the border which involve other currencies. It includes the trade figures mentioned above, which comprise net imports or exports (whichever is the greater) and the earnings (or losses) on what economists call 'invisibles' (although since 'invisibles' include earnings from tourism, I, in common with most Londoners, hardly class the visiting throngs that clog the public roads, parks and hotels as 'invisible'!). The 'invisibles' account also includes earnings from services like insurance, banking, shipping and other activities carried out abroad (or for payment by foreigners in their own currency) *minus* the same group of services and the like which we buy from them. The Government also looms large in this account, which includes, on the debit side, payments for British troops abroad and for our diplomatic missions – to the extent that they buy locally but not including goods sent out by the NAAFI and paid for in pounds – *minus* what foreign Governments spend here. All these added together make up the current account, which, as its name implies, measures the net current spending or earning of the nation in the rest of the world.

The next element is the capital account. This measures the flows, in and out, of money which is being moved to pay not for a current cost but for some other purpose. These other purposes are broadly two: direct investment and portfolio investment. We have seen a great deal of direct investment during the North Sea development, with foreign oil companies playing a direct part and spending their own money in setting up the oil terminals, pipelines and oil rigs. It is not just in the oil business that this sort of thing happens; innumerable foreign factories have been built in Britain. Chauvinists dislike what they see as the taking over of industry by foreign capital, but others welcome foreign investment, as it helps to create industry and jobs, even if in later years profits and dividends from those businesses may go abroad and turn up as outflows

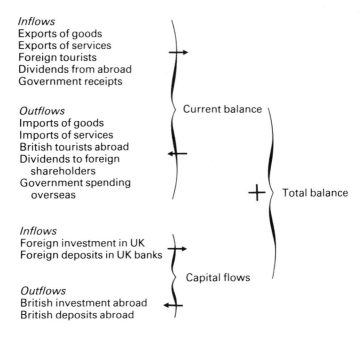

*In any year thousands of millions of pounds flow into and out of the country. The figure illustrates the 'flow' of the balance of payments, as a result of which there will have to be either an increase in Britain's official reserves of foreign currencies and gold (if the sum of the items on the left is the higher) or a decrease (if the total on the right is higher). The figure does not show the change in assets arising from, say, a British investment abroad that might be a benefit in years to come; such investment appears here as an outflow because it has to be paid for out of Britain's foreign currency earnings. Equally, while foreign investment in the UK appears here as an inflow, because the money comes into Britain, in fact such investment means that part of British capital is now in foreign hands.*

*Figure 3  Balance of payments*

on the current account. And the capital flows are not all one-way. For example, it was a well kept secret, for the sake of American *amour propre*, that when the largest American company, General Motors, moved its headquarters from Detroit to New York City the giant office block into which it moved at the corner of Central Park and Fifth Avenue was 51 per cent owned by a British property developer!

Capital exports of this kind often come in for criticism from people who would rather see the money 'stay at home' to provide jobs or wealth. But there can be – as with most economic observations – paradoxical effects. Thus although the Dunlop rubber company was heavily criticized, during the crisis of the European tyre industry, for having invested in plants abroad, one such investment turned up trumps. The company had bought the Sumitomo rubber company in Japan. When the tyre market came under great pressure in Britain because the car industry itself was producing far fewer new cars and hence needed fewer tyres in the first place – one reason for the slump in the British motor industry was the success of Japanese car makers in the British market place. But such was Sumitomo's success in Japan that more than half the imported cars coming into Britain had Dunlop tyres on them and therefore provided work for the labour force in British factories, replacing these tyres when they wore out – work which they would not have had without the initial investment years before in the Japanese plant.

All other investment is described as 'portfolio investment', which, as the name implies, includes the full variety of forms of investment that an individual or company can make. The portfolio may include stocks and shares, property or short-term deposits in banks or other financial institutions. Foreign investors may be attracted to make portfolio investments in Britain by opportunities for gain, by the level of interest rates or by the high level of stability, and therefore security, offered by British holdings.

Some of these capital flows are long-term, like the decision of the Kuwait Investment Agency in London to buy up the St

Martin's Property Company some years ago. That deal, made possible by the Arabs' sudden increase in oil wealth after the 1973 price increase, had the ironic side-effect of turning the strongly Arab protagonists into the landlords of one of the best-known Jewish enterprises in Britain, the Marks and Spencer store in Edgware Road. (No ideological tensions between landlord and tenant have been reported!)

Much more worry is expressed about short-term capital movements, the so-called 'hot money' which flows in and out of the world's financial centres. This 'hot money', running to thousands of millions of pounds, is made up of the loose cash which may at any time be available to private individuals or, more often, to company treasurers, bankers and other managers of large sums of money not tied up in long-term investment. Naturally, those who are charged with the management of large sums of cash, whether their own or others' placed in their trust, wish to maximize its security and, where possible, its earnings, and at any rate to avoid losses. It is widely felt that this money is put on deposit only to make the maximum amount for its owner, and not in the interests of the country concerned. But should a local authority treasurer, seeking funds to build a new town hall or repair the roads, spurn the deposit of an oil sheik or a German industrialist? It can be argued that the foreigner may suddenly remove his money, causing a 'run' out of London and leaving the borrowers who have been using the 'hot' money in difficulties.

This depends on the next stage of the process. What has gone before is a totting up of the total balance of payments, current and capital. At the end of the day (or month or year), there will have been a net inflow or outflow of foreign currency. In the jargon of the economists this is called the balance for official financing, which means the amount by which the country's stock of gold and foreign currencies has risen or fallen during the period. The official stocks of gold and foreign currency are held by the Bank of England as the reserves.

The money gets to the Bank of England as the result of the net transactions of all the traders and investors and *their* bankers. Thus, to take a simple example, if an exporter is paid $1 million for his sales to America, he will deposit those dollars with his bank and ask for sterling in exchange – after all, it is pounds, not dollars, that he will need to pay the wages, the dividends and all the other domestic costs. His bank will have thousands of other customers, some of whom may want dollars (for instance, if they import American goods or are going on trips to America). But eventually the bank will have a net sum – perhaps half the original million dollars – which it will deposit with the Bank of England, so adding to the official reserves, in exchange for sterling. It is the sum of all such transactions, public and private, current and capital (including sometimes payment of official national debts between Governments, like the repayment of various loans made by Britain during the Second World War), which increase or decrease the official reserves and from which can be gauged the absolute international performance of the whole economy.

As will be seen, the official reserves, consisting solely of foreign currency and gold, are themselves of great importance, and not just as a barometer of economic performance in foreign trade and payments. Their value lies in the capacity to buy foreign goods. In practice, most of the foreign goods imported into Britain are paid for from the proceeds of our own sales to foreign buyers, and over the years the two-way trade has kept remarkably close to balance. But there is always the possibility that for a shorter or longer period, we may fail to meet our needs out of export sales, and on these occasions the reserves can be used to buy essential foreign goods.

A recent example of the absolute necessity for holding reserves of foreign currency was the case of Nigeria, when in mid-1982 that oil-rich African country had to clamp down heavily on imports. The Nigerians were, quite simply, in danger of running entirely out of reserves because a fall in their (still large) oil revenues had caused their international income to drop below the monthly cost of imports for the large modernization programmes which they had initiated on the strength of their oil wealth. Having over-reached themselves in buying foreign materials, goods and machinery, and faced with the prospect of running out of money with which to pay, they simply had to call a halt before the reserves ran out completely. At times in the past, similar but, happily, less dramatic falls have been experienced by British reserves and those of other major trading countries.

As well as the 'ins' and 'outs' of reserve movements, there is also the crucial performance factor of the world value of the pound for trading. The reserves may go up or down, but what perhaps strikes the businessman more forcibly is what happens to the value of his pounds as an importer; for the exporter, the question is how expensive is his product going to be in foreign eyes when the value of the pound is taken into account?

Under the new dispensation – that is, since the 1971 changes described above – swings of value have tended to be much larger than before, but there has been much less worry about the movements up or down in the levels of the reserves. This is because of the methods used by the Bank of England in the management of the currency. In the pre-1971 fixed exchange rate days the Government, together with all other members of the IMF, undertook in the interests of international co-operation and stability to hold the value of the pound at a certain level (take $2.80) from 1949 to 1967. But how was this done, when trade worth millions of pounds a week was being carried on quite haphazardly between Britain and the rest of the world? Quite simply, the Bank, like any other bank, dealt in the market place.

In London the supply of foreign currency is handled by a number of specialist brokers, who will buy from or sell to any bank the foreign currencies it may have or may need for its customers. If there are more dollars about one day – as in the example above – the brokers will tend to lower their price for dollars and thus increase the price of pounds. Suppose, then, that the price of pounds moves towards $2.81. The Bank of England, acting as agent for government policy, must try to move the price back towards the agreed rate of $2.80. This it will do by telephoning the brokers and bidding for dollars. The brokers will sell dollars to the Bank in exchange for pounds but, the excess of dollars having gone, they will put their price back up again to $2.80. This technique is called 'intervention', and it was the method by which all the countries of the IMF nations kept their currencies at the agreed parities.

A crisis would come when, for instance, the balance of payments began to run in heavy loss, when for days on end there were more pounds about than dollars, and the Bank had to go on selling dollars into the market to keep the dollar value down (and the pound value up, of course). While the value of the pound would be maintained, the Bank would constantly be drawing on its reserves of dollars to make its intervention, and the old-fashioned sterling crisis would arise as the reserves dwindled to a dangerously low point.

To make matters worse, there would usually be a sort of band-wagon effect as other observers of the market saw the chance to make money if the value of the pound was forced down. So they too would sell pounds (which they had not got), hoping to buy them back later more cheaply.

This practice, known as 'dealing in the forward market', allows traders to buy or sell currencies ahead of the time when they will actually need the cash. Thus, for instance, an importer of German motor cars might wish to buy German marks for delivery on the day in perhaps one or three months' time when he will have to pay for the cars, rather than waiting until the future date. He is insuring against the possibility that the pound might fall compared with the mark over the next few weeks, making his imports more expensive. Equally, someone who knows in advance that he will be paid in marks for an export in three months' time might decide now to sell those marks forward, so that he has the cash in pounds now rather than later. In those hypothetical cases, if the mark rises, the importer will have done well and the exporter badly; on the other hand, the exporter will have benefited if the mark falls in the interval, since he would then have received fewer pounds at the end of the day if he had waited.

The forward market for currencies, administered by banks

and brokers in the City, emerged to meet the needs of traders but can be used by others who, though they have no strict need for money for trade, just wish to make profits by buying and selling currencies. It is these non-trading participants in the market who are known as 'speculators'. They form an important part of the mythology of the market and, by their selling of currencies 'forward', contribute to the fall in value of the currency under attack.

Before 1971 such attacks on the pound had to be parried. To stop the slide two things were normally done. The Government would announce measures – an important surcharge, a mini-Budget of tax and HP controls at home designed to reduce consumption – that would have a direct effect on the balance of payments. And to tide the Bank of England over the months it might take for these measures to have an effect on trade, an international loan of several thousand million dollars would be announced. The important thing about the loan was that it had to be big enough, and subscribed by enough of the right names, to convince the market that the pound was saved, from that crisis at any rate, and that there was therefore no case for selling.

As you will have noticed, in the midst of that account of an old-fashioned sterling crisis there was one element which impinged on the real economy: the package of measures designed to put things right. This meant that there was a direct connection between poor foreign trade, the fight to maintain the exchange rate and to stem the loss of reserves and the unpalatable medicine of higher purchase tax, HP controls and reduced prosperity. For those of you with long memories, this was the 'stop' in 'stop-go' economic policies.

Since 1971 the rules have changed. Poor trading performance no longer affects the economy through the same mechanical series of links. To begin with, there is no obligation on the Government to maintain any particular exchange rate for the pound versus the dollar for instance, so if more pounds than dollars are on offer in the market, the pound will sink in value against the American currency. Only if the Bank of England feels that things are moving too fast will it intervene. At other times the pound is allowed to 'float', and it has swung wildly, first downwards as Britain was running large balance of payments losses in the early 1970s, and then upwards as the richness of North Sea oil not only attracted foreign money on the capital account but later, when pumping began, replaced expensive imported oil and put the balance of payments into healthy surplus.

We have already seen how overseas performance affected the domestic economy when restrictive tax and credit measures had to be taken at home to defending a fixed exchange rate. In the new system the linkage is different. To start with, the 1979 Conservative Government rejected the idea of 'fine tuning' – that is, the changes in tax, interest rates and things like HP controls with which their predecessors had responded to the old-fashioned sterling crisis. But much more important is the change in the whole system to 'floating' exchange rates.

Broadly, the effect of a pound that is low against other currencies is to push prices up at home – not surprisingly, considering that a quarter of all that we buy for consumption and industry comes from abroad, and therefore each item reflects in its price the pound's own value against the currency of the country of origin, be it Japanese yen, German mark or French franc. But a low pound is also expected to help British industry because it reduces the price of British exports and therefore makes them more attractive to foreign buyers.

One of the dilemmas of modern economic practice is which of these two effects is the more important. As higher prices are fairly rapidly translated into higher wages by the tough transmission of wage demands through collective bargaining, industry finds itself facing higher costs and the need to put up prices, which somewhat modifies the benefit of the lower pound. On the other hand, too high a pound may damage exports permanently. To counter that, a high pound reduces the rate of price increase because imports become less expensive, and they are an important component in the cost of living. But, as many commentators pointed out during the period of high value for the pound in the early 1980s, the benefit through inflation may be offset by disadvantages in real trade. Exports, as mentioned above, may be lost, and imports will increase as foreign goods become cheaper than their home-made equivalents.

It is virtually impossible to fix a perfect exchange rate, one which truly reflects value for money in transactions going both ways across the border. This, of course, is partly why the old stable exchange rate system finally collapsed: no one could agree on the perfect rate for the dollar and other major currencies. One reason is that different countries experience different rates of inflation and therefore changes in their export prices. It would be impossible to maintain an identical exchange rate indefinitely between a country like Germany, with inflation running at below 5 per cent, and France, with an annual increase in prices that is more than double that figure.

If stability is for the moment unattainable, what most affects the general economic scene may be not the rate on any particular day but the impact on economic activity of the big changes which take place in the value of the currency. Thus Britain lost competitiveness very rapidly *vis-à-vis* her major trading partners after the period of the late 1970s in which high wage settlements, high manufacturing costs and a weak pound had reflected accurately her ability to sell abroad. When for extraneous reasons – the oil, for instance – the pound started its sharp rise, it took a year or more for wage cost increases to slow down, and British industry had the mortifying experience of having to charge prices based on wages which were still rising fast in cash terms and then having to add on yet more (or take less profit) when selling abroad on account of the rising pound.

Under both systems, then, damage can be done to the real economy at home by poor performance abroad. It would be presumptuous to judge between the ill effects of the 'stop' of 'stop-go' and the equally debilitating effects of an over-strong pound on manufacturing industry in recent years. In either case the country's domestic industry is 'blown off course' (to use the phrase of Ted Heath in the early 1970s) by external affairs. But it would be ducking the issue not to reflect that during the period 1950–70, when the major industrial nations operated with fixed exchange rates and intervened to maintain them, the world enjoyed a growth of prosperity in real terms and came closer to combining full employment with sound money (that is to say, lack of inflation) than at any time since 1914. Since 1971 and the abandonment of the attempt to hold exchange rates steady a marked worsening has been monitored by the main economic barometers. Unemployment has risen throughout the industrial West; the erosion of money values has accelerated to horrific proportions; imbalances between countries' balances of payments have become vaster; and the world has become an uncomfortably jittery place where no one can predict with reliable conviction a return to the prosperous years.

It is argued both that we should blame the Organization of Petroleum Exporting Countries (OPEC) oil crisis, not the breakdown of the fixed exchange rate system, for the present recession and also that in any case the old system, with its reliance on the stock of international reserves for steadying currency rates, could not have coped with the storm of quin-tupled oil prices which followed so soon after its collapse. But arguments do not dislodge the fact that the going is rougher under the new regime than it was under the old and that the troubles of the industrial West now make one wonder what all the fuss was about when we had the far less damaging, though at the time frustrating, bouts of 'stop' in the 1950s and 1960s.

Before concluding this chapter on international trade one more aspect needs to be mentioned. We have seen the effects that private movements of money can have on the economy; there is also the impact of foreign institutions which have a bearing on the country through foreign trading. The most important, for Britain, is the IMF, whose influence on Mr Roy Jenkins's famous tough Budget of 1968 is described in chapter 1.

The IMF is notorious for its interference in the domestic

affairs of its member countries, and politicians have made much of 'the men from the IMF' who dictate British policy when it suits their book. In essence, the Fund is a bank to which all the countries of the non-Communist world have subscribed contributions in gold and their own currencies so that any one or more of them can borrow money to meet a crisis, but it lends only to countries whose problems arise abroad – that is, its loans are to cover only foreign debts, not, the construction of new schools or hospitals, for instance.

The reason why it is often described as influencing policy (or worse) is that much of its lending is conditional. A member can borrow a fixed proportion of its subscription without conditions, but if it goes above that limit, as Britain did in 1967, then it must meet certain conditions, and these may entail trimming its own domestic economic policies. These conditions, the Fund says, are designed for one end alone, to enable the country concerned to earn back, in its foreign trade, the money that it has borrowed from the Fund. Repayment is normally scheduled for between three and five years after the initial borrowing, so sometimes the medicine has to be quite drastic if the loan is large. A case in point in 1982–3 has been the conditions that the Mexican Government has been asked to meet to ensure that it will be able to repay its latest crisis borrowing from the IMF.

Critics of the Fund say that its restrictions are too conservative. Mr Michael Manley, the Prime Minister of Jamaica, actually refused to meet the IMF's conditions for a loan in the late 1970s, though the long-run consequences of his almost unique rejection of the terms have not been tested, since his Government fell at the subsequent elections, and his decision was reversed by his successors.

The second important international institution to which the major trading nations of the world belong is the Geneva-based General Agreements on Tariffs and Trade (GATT), the body which supervises negotiations to keep world trade as free as possible from deliberate barriers like quotas, tariffs or other forms of protectionism. Over the years GATT has sought through the agreement of members, to reduce the trade barriers which have sprung up from time to time. It has produced various codes of practice, including, for instance, the rules which allow one member to discriminate against the products of another if it can show with absolute certainty that these goods are being 'dumped' on its market ('Dumping' means that the exporting concern is getting a subsidy or other help from official sources which allows it to sell its manufactures abroad at a price which is actually lower than the cost of production or, in the case of raw materials and commodities, below the Free World price.) GATT also supervises many other forms of tariff-barrier, such as the EEC's external tariff, which is discussed in the next chapter.

Finally, Britain is a member of the Organization for Economic Co-operation and Development (OECD). The OECD, based in Paris, is a group of the two dozen wealthiest non-Communist industrial countries. It does not have the clout of the IMF – simply because it does not fulfil a banking role, which would oblige those who borrow to stick to its prescriptions – but the committees of officials and Ministers who regularly meet at the OECD do try to agree on the least damaging strategies that they can pursue.

One of the matters that they discuss is interest rates. Throughout 1981 and 1982 the OECD members were urging the United States to bring down the level of her interest rates and thus to reduce the magnetic upward pull that these were exerting on European rates. It is not possible to measure exactly what influences carried most weight with the Americans, but by the end of 1982 they were attempting to get rates down: and that is just the sort of domestic policy with an international effect which the OECD deals with.

The Organization offers one other important advantage to the reader of this book. Each year it produces a report on its member countries' economic performances, and these 'country reports' from OECD provide a very useful, and comparatively simple, snapshot of the state of the various major industrial countries, including Britain. Twice a year the OECD also produces an 'economic outlook' for the whole group, which is probably the best such guide to the direction and state of economic health of the richest – but at the moment far from the healthiest – group of countries in the world.

# 14

## International Relations

Chapter 13 attempted to outline the context in which the economy operates in foreign trade and other dealings. The environment was transformed by the financial events of the 1970s. The collapse of the post-war co-operative fixed exchange rate system and the oil shocks of 1973–4 and 1979. There are other ways in which the international scene has been changing and on which decision-takers have to keep a close watch.

For Britain the most important change in recent years has been her membership of the EEC. An enormous number of decisions have to be taken nowadays with an eye on Brussels as well as on domestic markets and the home Government.

The EEC, which now includes ten nations (Britain joined, with Ireland and Denmark, when the first six had already been together for about fifteen years, and Greece followed some years later), is primarily political in inspiration but is held together at institutional and bureaucratic levels by economic regimes. Of these the two most important are the Common Agricultural Policy (CAP), a system for maintaining the income of the European agricultural producers through high price levels, and the Community Budget – much of which is spent on the CAP.

Important to any understanding of the EEC is that the essential parts of these two economic regimes are automatic. Thus the funds contributed to the central Community Budget are largely remitted without the day-to-day discretion of any member country and through the automatic working of agreed duties and tariffs. These fund-raising devices are twofold.

First, the Common External Tariff (CET), which is levied on manufactured and other goods imported by any EEC country from anywhere outside the EEC. This CET (of about 7 per cent) is collected at the frontiers of EEC countries by customs officers and sent straight to Brussels, without discretion, by the collecting country. Second, the food levy. This system requires each country to charge importers of foods produced inside the EEC a sum equal to the difference between world prices and the Community's own prices for such foods. (This does not cover everything, of course: there are no Community prices for bananas because no bananas are grown in the EEC, so no levy is payable on the import of such foods.)

Some of the most important food levies are on beef, sugar and dairy products. They mean, in broad terms, that shoppers buying these foods, whether grown in the Community or imported from outside at lower world prices, pay the same prices in the shops. (This is done, along with other regulations on quantity as well as price, to prevent people from shopping around to find goods produced more cheaply than in Europe. The measure is part of the policy that aims to enrich the European agricultural population.) It will quickly be seen that the amount of food levies collected will be determined by the gap between world and EEC prices, and thus this very important part of EEC Budget income is heavily influenced by the annual decision of the Community farming Ministers on what the prices to European farmers should be.

We come now to the other side of the EEC equation: the spending side. Something over 70 per cent of the income of the Community is spent on the CAP, which seems surprising, since the central part of the policy is to set food prices high so that consumers will pay the farmers a living wage. However, the system is operated in a way which places a large burden on the central budget, as follows.

Once the prices have been agreed at the annual price review, the officials of the Community arrange 'intervention' to buy any quantities of, for instance, beef, milk or butter which would otherwise, at normal market prices, fall below the 'intervention' price. If the price has been set too high, the authorities may find farmers offering unduly large quantities of meat or dairy products, which then have to be bought in to prevent the market price from falling. All this costs a great deal, and to the actual 'intervention' buying (which, incidentally, holds prices in the shops up to the EEC level even when world prices are lower) must be added the cost of storage of the surpluses produced.

Eventually some of this surplus food may be sold outside the EEC (the sale of butter to the Russians is the most notorious, because politically most irritating, of such deals) but only at world prices. When such sales are often described as 'subsidized', this is a misleading description. Having decided to run a system of pricing and intervention which obliges them to buy large quantities of milk and dairy products from their own farmers, at fixed prices, in order to maintain farm incomes, the authorities then find themselves holding large stocks of over-produced goods. To sell these inside the Community would defeat the whole purpose of the exercise by depressing the price and making the farmers poor once more, so they are sold outside the Community. Any proceeds from these sales actually reduce the cost to the system of the CAP, so far from the sales to Russia being 'subsidized', it is the proceeds from these sales, at or near the world price, which themselves subsidize the Common Market Budget!

There are other hideous complexities in the Common Market system which need not concern us, but one more, the 'export rebate', is important. This is a sum of money paid to an EEC farmer who exports outside the Community and receives a payment which will bring the world price he gets up to the higher EEC price.

The interaction of these provisions produces the inequities about which the British Government has been complaining almost ever since Britain became a member of the Community. It is an over-simplification, but not a gross one, to blame the structure of the EEC Budget and the CAP for the fact that Britain and West Germanty pay large net contributions into the Community Budget while most other members pay nothing at all or receive net subsidies.

As described above, the main sources of Community income, automatically gathered, are the CET on manufactured goods (items like cars and consumer goods, of which Britain has always been a large importer from outside Europe) and the food levies, which bring the price of commodities like New Zealand lamb and butter up to EEC prices at the point of entry. Both these sources of revenue to the Community Budget bear heavily on Britain. In exchange, however, she receives rather less from the two major areas of expenditure in the Budget – intervention buying of British farm products and export rebates – than other countries, and this simply because as an industrialized country her farming sector is relatively small (occupying about 3 per cent of the labour force) and as a net importer of food she is unlikely to benefit from export rebates. And while more than 70 per cent of the Community Budget is spending on the farm regime, the remainder is used for social, regional and industrial purposes, and from these funds Britain does a little better.

However, while the cost of running the CAP consumes the lion's share of the Budget, countries like Britain and Germany, which are heavily industrialized and heavily engaged in trade outside the Community, are inevitably the losers in budget contributions. It has been suggested that the EEC Budget would be better divided between schemes that would help the industrialized countries and those that would assist the farming ones: but any such suggestions run into a complex road block. The size of EEC spending on the CAP is determined largely by the level of Community farm prices and consequent butter mountains, wine lakes, etc. The Community's income is made up of non-discretionary levies on food and manufactured goods imports. In addition, each country contributes a sum of money (from its own Budget) equivalent to a value added tax of 1 per cent to make up the total sum available for all Community projects.

If, as the British Government would like, more money were

spent on regional and industrial development or subsidies (as on farm subsidy already), the whole Community Budget would have to be enlarged. But the very countries who might benefit from a wider spread of Community spending – in the sense that they would get back more of the money they put in and would reduce their 'net' contributions – are wholly opposed to any enlargement of the Budget, which under present conventions would be possible only by increasing the 'VAT element' from a sum equivalent to 1 per cent to one equivalent to 1.5 or 2 per cent.

(I keep saying 'sum equivalent to' a VAT levy of 1 per cent to make it clear that the contribution is not, in the British case at least, taken from VAT payments. It is, in fact, paid from the general revenues of Government, but the maximum amount payable is computed from the yield of a notional 1 per cent VAT. The distinction is important because the notional VAT on which the computation is based applies to food and other goods which attract no VAT in Britain. Further, the 1 per cent computation is the maximum; what is actually paid is based on what has been spent by the Community. So far the 'VAT element' has always been below the limit, but talk of a Budget crisis in the Community often refers to the possibility that if the Eurocrats set food prices too high, thus increasing CAP costs, or in other ways spent too much money, the members would have to pay up more than the 'VAT ceiling' and might jib at so doing. Then the retrenchment and recriminations would be something to be seen; compared with them the recent arguments over the Budget and members' shares would be seen to be a minor skirmish.)

Analysis of the EEC Budget is only one facet of a debate in British politics which goes a great deal deeper than the argument over 'net contributions' and touches the very question whether Britain should be in the EEC at all – whether the Community is itself a 'good' or a 'bad' thing for Britain. It has been estimated that the 'true' cost to Britain of membership is perhaps double the size of net Budget contributions or even more. This, it is argued, is because food prices – which have to be paid by the customer – are higher than they would otherwise be, so that the national cost is higher than the official cost of being in the Community system. Even so, and even if the 'true' cost had been the £2,000 million-odd estimated by critics of the EEC in 1980, this sum is only about 1 per cent of total national income. While the arguments are vehement, the sums changing hands are relatively small in the context of the whole economy.

There was, however, fierce argument in the early years of British membership about the trading advantages or dis-advantages of membership. Proponents argued that British traders would do even better once Britain was in the EEC; a few years later opponents argued that since we had joined European goods had flooded into Britain (not the other way round), and our industry had suffered, not prospered, through membership. In its latest form the argument advanced is that if Britain were to withdraw, she would somehow 'lose' the very large export markets which industry enjoys in Europe.

All these arguments over-simplify; and crude over-simplification of the case by pro- and anti-Marketeers has made it much more difficult for the inquiring layman to under-stand this aspect of economic life.

Let us glance back at the early 1970s, before Britain joined the EEC, when the Conservative Government published a White Paper arguing 'the economic case for British entry' and even produced a simplified version to be given away free at all Post Offices. Shortly afterwards a full-page advertisement appeared in *The Times*, subscribed to by a vast list of names in politics and industry, even a handful of trade unionists. Most of the page was taken up with the list of names, but pride of place was given to a quotation from the 'pop' version of the White Paper which read: 'When Britain joins the Common Market, British industry will have a home market six times as large as at present.'

Here the Establishment was well and truly fibbing. By no stretch of the imagination – or the scope conventionally accorded to politicians to extend the facts of economic life to suit their argument – could it be said that the nine countries of the EEC were about to become a 'home market' on Britain's accession. Common sense tells one that a 'home market' is one that possesses, first and foremost, a single currency: the pound, the dollar, the franc or what have you. Once you have to exchange from one into another, bang goes your 'home market', and you're in foreign trade.

Well, you may argue, this is just nit-picking. They did not really *mean* 'home market' (and in fact the official White Paper, as opposed to the 'pop' version, did not use the phrase); what they meant was a 'free trade area' with no tariffs or barriers to trade between members. But the benefit of the doubt does not let the authors of the phrase, and those who heartily endorsed it in *The Times*, off the hook, for Britain was already a member of the European Free Trade Area (EFTA) outside the EEC, and while the 'free trade area' of the Community, with a population of about 300 million, might be described (roughly) as 'six times as large' as the United Kingdom's home market, it was only about one and a half times as large as the EFTA population of about 450 million. And anyone who hoped that the 'home market' argument would bring the sort of convenience that truly domestic trading brings must be sorely disappointed, as the fluctuations in the relative values of the pound against the German mark and French franc since Britain joined have been far larger (in both directions) than the changes in tariffs granted to Britain on joining the Community.

Anti-EEC arguments may be equally fatuous. Those who say, for instance, Britain's membership falsely directs British trade and investment in Europe away from our older trading partners in the Commonwealth and North America conveniently neglect the truth that one of the greatest boosts to British trading in Europe – and especially direct investment in European markets and concerns – took place not after we joined but in the earlier decade following General de Gaulle's 'Non', when Britain was kept out for political reasons but on the commercial and business front British entrepreneurs were determined to get into the vast market on the doorstep.

Perhaps, to sum up, the EEC should not be allowed to assume too large a significance, as bane or benefit, in our economic life. In the past ten years there has been a large expansion in Euro–British trade (reducing the proportion of total trade with North America). At first most of the increase was in British imports from Europe, so the trade balance worsened. Latterly that trend has reversed, and as Britain's overall trading position has improved, so she has moved into surplus *vis-à-vis* the rest of the EEC. It would be difficult to imagine Britain 'losing' her trade with Europe: but in any case that would not follow from a political withdrawal from the institutions of the EEC and the Treaty of Rome. The vast bulk of the trade would (in what seems, at the time of writing, to be an extraordinarily remote contingency) continue. To be sure, British exporters would be 'outside' the CET wall, but the price disadvantage that would impose (of less than 10 per cent) would be far less than the worsening (of about 30 per cent) in Britain's competitiveness with the major trading partners in Europe which has marked the last dozen years, as British costs and prices have risen much faster than those in Germany and other EEC countries. Compared with these major influences on Britain's world trade, the technical aspects of Community membership are slight, though the psychological ones of being in rather than out are probably very much more important. Because a great deal of the argument about the 'cost' or the 'benefits' of Europe are argued in economic terms, the narrowly economic balance may be given too much importance compared with the wider political, strategic and cultural reasons for being in or out of Europe.

# 15

# Local Authorities

Next only to the general health of the economy – measured by reference to unemployment, inflation and taxation – the most important influence in everyday economic life is wielded by local authorities. Yet understanding local authority finance and the way in which decisions are made in local government are among the most complicated of matters.

Local authorities raise money in three ways: by rents from council house dwellers, by rates from industrial, commercial and domestic property, and from central Government funds. They also borrow money, both directly from the public and through the Public Works Loans Board. Local authority treasurers use the City of London to borrow long-term and, through a brisk market in local authority debt, can also borrow for as little as a few months or weeks or even, in the short-term money markets, overnight.

The money thus raised is spent on housing, education, health, roads and transport and local social services. In the local authority spending game there is a continuous four-way tug of war between customers for local authority services, ratepayers, council tenants and, of course, central government. In the struggle for decent services, low rates and government money there is also the distortion produced by the fact of life that some areas are richer than others and that, paradoxically, the former will tend to have higher income from rates but less demanding needs to meet. In other areas the problem will be precisely the reverse: low income from rates but higher than average needs for social services and other amenities. Decaying inner cities are often examples of the latter category, suburban or rural areas of the former.

So far as the observer of the economy is concerned, there is not a great deal of information available to help one to pick one's way through the complexities of local authority decision-taking, though at the local level there is often a fair amount of debate and argument in the press.

Before going into the mechanisms which govern local authority decision-taking, it is worth setting out a few principles. The purpose of local and regional government is evidently to allow the decisions which have most immediate local impact to be taken by locally elected councils of local people, supported by their own separate bureaucracy locally recruited and based. From parish council rows about footpaths across newly ploughed fields to great clashes of political weight about such issues as the retention of the 11-plus examination, local authorities have considerable independence and power.

Their influence on the economy can be extremely local – they can decide to build a by-pass to avoid a shopping street or vary local by-laws for innkeepers or tradesmen – or much wider, as in the case of the efforts that some local councils have made either to preserve jobs in the public sector by using direct labour for building and road schemes or to sacrifice them by, for instance, putting such work as rubbish collection out to private tender.

There can also be political rows, in which the party colour of the council becomes inextricably entwined with the practical issues of local spending and fund raising. The famous cases of the Clay Cross councillors in Derbyshire, who were eventually penalized for their wage and rate policies, only to be retrospectively forgiven with the change from a Conservative to a Labour Government in 1974, is one such case, and the Greater London Council's 'Fares Fair' campaign to cut public transport fares and load the subsidy on to London ratepayers was conceived and executed by a Labour council for socialist and electoral reasons.

However, setting aside ideological battle cries, there are one or two vital rules that govern local authority economic behaviour. While local authorities are given considerable autonomy within certain areas of responsibility such as the spending of money, they are not given anything like such freedom to raise money. They do not have powers to tax individuals other than through the rates, and, as the London Transport case showed, they do not have complete freedom to vary the charges they make. And one very important general principle emerged into the light of day (though it had always been known to the experts) after the House of Lords' decision that the London Transport fares could not be subsidized excessively by the ratepayers, and that was that local authorities have no power to do anything that is not expressly permitted them by Parliament. In spite of universal suffrage for local elections, the democratically elected members of local authorities are elected to do only the tasks specifically allocated to them by the senior democratically elected body in the land.

This constitutional provision also has a good deal of influence over the economics of local government and the way in which town halls can run their affairs. The power vested in central government resides not only in its constitutional authority to license local authority activities through Acts of Parliament (it was the London Transport Act which tripped up the Greater London Council in the fares case) but also in the fact that it controls the purse strings. About 60 per cent of all local authority money comes from central government; the provision of taxpayers' money to town halls is made, broadly, in exchange for the duties carried out by law by the local authorities.

The importance of the local authorities' dependence on London for funds is evident. It gives central government two distinct fields in which to direct, or even to discipline, local authority spending. The first is the overall control of the total amount of money spent by town halls in the whole economy. This control can be exercised by varying the amount of the Rate Support Grant (RSG), which is the proper title of the cash paid over to councils out of the Exchequer. To a certain extent, councils can try to get round changes in the RSG by using other sources of funds – for instance, by increasing their rates if the announced RSG is less than they feel they need to keep services going. However, recently the Government has assumed powers to penalize individual authorities and to prevent them from getting round a lower support grant by raising rates faster. The penalty is incurred when the local authority *spends* what the Department of the Environment judges to be too much. It may then find its 'block grant' cut back, so that higher spending based on higher rates can be inhibited by the withholding of some government money. This may have the effect that services and total spending have to be cut back even while local rates are increased, placing the local ratepayer in the worst of all possible worlds, but the intention of the new scheme is to discourage the over-spending which can lead to higher rates in the first place.

The second line of fire, so to speak, of the annual RSG settlement – a day of dread for borough treasurers – is the redistribution of grant for political, historical or economic reasons. One year the weight of grant support may be shifted to favour large urban councils; another year it may be tilted to help the county authorities. Losers in the annual round will always cry 'politics'. Winners tend to keep their mouths shut in the hope that their luck will not change next time round.

From the foregoing it is evident that Government can have a very forceful impact on local authority economics at many levels. The student of local authority money needs to keep a sharp eye on the RSG settlements once a year, followed in the spring by the announcements, across the country, of new rating levels. Within the community of ratepayers there is also the rivalry between domestic and industrial rates. The CBI is a source of information about the burden of business rates and frequently campaigns for these to be reduced or at least not to rise so fast.

So far I have dwelt on local authority fund raising, not so much on information about their spending. The key issues for economy watchers here are wages and services. Each year there are large national negotiations for the main groups of workers employed by local authorities – teachers, firemen, the police, social workers, (and in the sub-branch, separately paid for, water and sewage workers). Since some of these groups are recognized nationally for the purpose of wage bargaining (the police, notably, and the teachers), the local authorities feel the consequences of wage settlements, for good or ill, without always being able to influence the negotiations. On the other hand, there are also groups of local authority employees who deal with negotiating committees representing all local authorities, or sub-groups within the total, through their own nationally organized trades unions.

Squeezed between the upper millstone of government influence over, if not direct control of, their income and the nether millstone of nationally negotiated wage settlements (wages representing by far the largest share of their total budgets), the local authorities have to do the best they can to provide for their communities those services which will get the party in power reelected at the next election. It is not surprising, therefore, that local authority organizations are sceptical (to say the least) of central government. What is more, that central government lays specific duties – in connection with education, policing, the fire service, health care – on local authorities. The result is that their room for manoeuvre, should their budgets be under pressure, is limited either to economies in the non-statutory services that they provide – parks, recreation, cleansing (one dustbin collection a week instead of two in commercial areas?) – or to cutting to the minimum staff and amenities in the obligatory sectors of their work.

Local authorities are the poor relation in debates about public spending and finance, not least because their methods of funding are complicated and highly regulated. However, in spite of their relatively obscure place in the general economic debate, the finances of the local authorities and their spending programmes are vital to the general health of the whole economy, partly because they spend between them so large a share of total public expenditure. As we have seen, they have

,relatively little control over the total sums spent, but because these are so large, and because more than half of all sums spent by local authorities comes from central funds, the tail of the local authority may often seem to be wagging the dog of Downing Street and the Treasury.

Equally, though on a smaller scale, local decisions locally arrived at about schooling, street lighting or council housing have vital ramifications for local people, both because they colour the services provided and because they affect the level of rates paid by every household and industry. Endless discussion about reforming the rates system seems to have got no nearer to generally acceptable alternatives (local income taxes, sales taxes or other substitutes for the current property taxation) but reflects the continuing concern of politicians and rate- and rent-payers to improve the giant machinery of local government spending.

# 16

## State Industries

Chapter 15 dealt with the fund-raising and spending problems of local authorities: but these are by no means the only big spenders in the public sector discussed in chapter 8. The other giants on the public scene are the state industries: railways, coal, steel, gas, electricity, the post, telecommunications, oil, shipbuilding, computers and aerospace.

All these activities differ from local government in that the vast bulk of their revenue comes from sales (whereas local authorities draw a very small part of their total income from rents and charges). The accounts of the National Coal Board, British Rail, British Steel, the Post Office or British Telecom, show that they succeed in covering the largest proportion – sometimes even the whole – of their costs from sales of the services they provide.

Nonetheless, too many state industries too often run into financial trouble which, in the private sector of industry, would drive them out of business. The Government bails them out for a wide variety of reasons. British Rail has its losses met year after year because a national railway network is regarded as part of the social framework provided by the state. Sir Peter Parker, as Chairman of British Rail, liked to draw a distinction between the 'commercial railway' and the 'social railway'. So far as he was concerned, the only difference between providing the 'commercial railway' (Inter-City services and freight, on which he could make money) and the 'social railway' (commuter services into London and other cities, and some remote rural services, on which he could not) was that the end-customer was different. If, he implied, society wanted commuter rail networks and rural railways on which office clerks or farm labourers could not afford to travel out of their own pockets, then subsidies should be openly provided, by national or local government, to the loss-making services. In such cases the customer was not just the traveller but also the state, representing society in its wish that transport should be provided.

In a sense, Sir Peter encapsulates much of the debate about publicly owned corporations – the Post Office, for instance – and how they should be expected to operate. In some cases the reasons for state ownership are strategic: the British National Oil Corporation (BNOC) was formed to take an interest in the newly discovered North Sea oil deposits because the Government of the day wanted to play a part in North Sea oil development. The public sale, in late 1982, of Britoil, which ran much of BNOC's operating interests in finding and selling the oil, still left the state-owned BNOC with the strategic powers that the Government felt it needed for North Sea oil development.

But if the oil case was strategic, the ownership of coal mining and steel making in Britain passed into the hands of the state for political reasons. Unlike the cases of the railway network or the Royal Mail, there was no suggestion that the consumer of these services was owed them, that they met a social need. Nor was the post-war nationalization of coal and steel undertaken for strategic reasons, as was the control of North Sea oil. The nationalizations were carried out in accordance with the political ideal that the principal means of production and supply should be owned collectively by society, not by private interests, whether 'private' in the sense of a few multi-millionaire entrepreneurs or 'private' in the sense of tens of thousands of shareholders.

Apart from this diversity of origin, the state industries enjoy widely different contexts in which to operate. Some are effectively monopolies (the electricity boards, the water authorities); others face limited competition (the Post Office competes with messenger services in towns and cities); and some face virtually free competition (British Rail competes for traffic with road hauliers, British Steel with foreign steel, the Coal Board not only with imported coal but also with oil and gas as domestic and industrial fuels). By no means all of the state industries enjoy the feather bed of monopoly, though most are shielded from the fiercest open competition, if only because of a general feeling that, being state-owned, they will never be allowed to fail. Perhaps in future this view will be truly tested by concerns like Rolls-Royce and British Leyland, which were taken into public ownership in order to be saved but which both strive in a fiercely competitive industry. Rolls-Royce at least has the safety net of its defence equipment business, which manufactures engines for Harriers and other military planes – a net, however, which has already once, in 1971, obliged the Government to step in to save the bankrupt company. Leyland has no such safety net – only the frailer notion of national prestige and, during the current recession, the importance to Governments of preserving jobs in the vast motor industry in order to supplement its competitive capacity.

The various state enterprises are nevertheless important to their customers, to their employees and to the economy as a whole. The decisions taken by managers in state industries are far from simple. The managers are not only required to meet the non-commercial objectives of their organizations, be they social provisions or strategic considerations but also to respond to what can be mercurial political direction from government. Whatever the reasons why the nation's coal mines, British Leyland or the aero-engine business of Rolls-Royce fell into the hands of the state, now that they are there they are subject to the changing whims of changing administrations in Whitehall and Westminster.

Imperial Chemical Industries (ICI), for many years Britain's largest manufacturing company, had a planning committee of very senior managers and directors. According to its terms of reference, that planning committee was not allowed to consider any change due in less than five years' time. The point of that instruction was that for a company of ICI's complexity and size, any major change due within five years must have already moved on from the 'planning' stage to action in the operating divisions of the company. Managers of nationalized industries complain that they are seldom allowed that detachment in their planning, since their plans are often overturned by government Departments whose policy for state industries may change rapidly.

Examples of this sort of interference from above include the series of steep gas price increases for domestic users in the early 1980s. The Energy Department insisted on higher gas prices, even though British Gas was making plenty of money, in order artificially to bring gas more closely into line with other energy sources. This move in turn was linked to a general policy of trying to save energy, but it ran counter to the Government's otherwise declared aim of leaving prices to market forces. On the other hand, a proposed rise in telephone charges was abandoned after public protests – British Telecom was also making large profits – through the influence of the Government.

Partly as a result of these and other artificial influences, and partly for the simple reason that they are so large, the state industries play a disproportionately important role in economic developments nationally.

They are, in the first place, greedy for funds. Operating on a national scale, their appetite for investment cash is very large and therefore very vulnerable whenever a Government decides that capital projects must be restrained so as to reduce total borrowing and interest rates. Public borrowing, whether by state industries or by the local authorities whose current spending was discussed in chapter 15, attracts the tight control of the Government; and it is conceivable, though not I think proven, that were these great enterprises to be split into smaller groups, so that they were no longer beholden, as a collection of nationalized corporations, to a single authority for permission to borrow, they might not find themselves staggering from expansion to contraction and back again quite as briskly as they have under successive Governments in recent years.

The other main impact which the nationalized industries

have on economic life is in the arena of wage bargaining. For many years until 1981 or 1982 there had been a feeling that employees of state industries were distinct from their counterparts in the private sector. At the back of the minds of trade unionists, commentators and politicians lurked the conviction that, because of their very nature, state industries could not be 'let go'.

Because the state industries in Britain employ such a relatively large number of workers (as compared, say, with America, Japan or Germany), the successive wage rounds in the late 1960s and 1970s, in which these employees won hefty wage increases, had a considerable effect on the rest of the labour force. This sequence may well have contributed to the very rapid rise in money incomes (closely followed by rising prices at home, so its main effect was not to secure higher living standards but to produce higher unit costs in international trade) which came to an end only in 1981–2. Then the Government's determination not to concede high money wage increases was emphasized by the programme of 'privatization', which suggested that such concerns, if they were not to be 'let go', were at least to be released to cruise under their own steam. The Government's stand was consolidated by the severity of the domestic recession and by unemployment above the 3 million level.

For whatever reason, one state concern after another agreed money wage settlements at very low levels in 1982. Indeed, some were so low that wages were not protected against the impact of price increases, though these had also slowed down during the recession. In these cases the Government, assisted by the chill winds of recession and unemployment, saw its objective of lower pay settlements carried through. Although the coalminers' pay award of 8.5 per cent was more than twice what the Government would have liked to see, the majority of 60 to 40 by which the miners rejected the idea of industrial action to improve the offer showed most clearly the way in which economic reality was impinging on a great nationalized industry.

A final thought on the impact of these giants and their significance in national wage bargaining and price setting (for many of them are monopolies, too). Perhaps their very size, the example they set and the considerable national attention which is accorded to them may actually have slowed down the response of the British economy to the crisis of 1979. Certainly, the reactions of both restraining pay and price increases and improving output per man by reducing employment came much more quickly in the private sector. And it may well be that this slimming down in order to become more effective in trading happened more readily in the private sector because the units are in general much smaller and the motives of the companies less mixed. They are less burdened by political or social issues, and government departments breathe less down their necks.

# PART III

# Individual Decisions

# 17

# Personal Finance

So far this book has explored the decisions made by politicians and the managers of the economy, whether in industry or in government, local, national or even international. By far the most important, these are the decisions which rule our lives – or rather, they rule the climate of life in which individuals prosper or founder.

The remaining chapters are going to attempt a more difficult, but I hope worthwhile, charting of the economy: that is, the thousands of millions of individual decisions which are not only exceptionally important in driving the economy but, more to the point, are taken by individuals ostensibly in their own interests. They do not always result in the desired ends; they are often perverse (like the fact that people save more when money is losing value fastest.)

I have left these multitudinous sorts of decision to last because this book does not aim in any way to be a guide to behaviour. I cannot make you a million pounds – if I could, I would not be writing these words – and I am certainly not an adviser of any kind on personal finances. Nonetheless, making sense of the economy must include making sense of the personal budget as well as the national one. There is no lack of information, but, as in the case of so many economic issues, the problem is interpreting it.

Doctors and financial advisers have one thing in common. In financial decision-making, as in the treatment of ailments, there are myriad combinations of personal circumstance which make generalized advice likely to be slightly wrong for almost everyone, even if it is precisely right for someone. Equally, a very large array of choices faces the individual at any moment, and matching the right product to the customer is as difficult in the context of financial management as it is when you set out to buy a Christmas present for a finicky teenager. Picking your way through economic choices of this sort is evidently going to be difficult, but at least there are some basic guides and signposts.

It is a sad but undeniable fact that people often fail to act in their own best interests. The most marked manifestation of this human failing is the behaviour of small investors in the stock market. What they do, in a nutshell, is to buy at the top and sell at the bottom. The psychology of this behaviour is explicable, even if the rationality of it is not.

When the stock market is falling and the FT Index is drifting downwards, people with a little spare cash tend to be worried in case the market falls further, and the further it falls, the less inclined are they to buy. But when the market is rising fast, when the newspapers are full of stories about share rises and 'record levels' of the various indexes and share markets, then small investors tend to be enthusiastic buyers of shares. This is true not just of people investing directly in shares but also, perhaps even more, of savers buying the ready-made investments offered for sale by unit trusts.

These trusts, in effect, buy a wide range of shares in the stock market and then sell to the private investor a unit of the whole portfolio. It saves the individual investor the trouble of working out for himself what to buy or sell at any time, and it promises both the expertise of the fund managers and the relative safety of the spreading of risk through a large number of shares. Units in unit trusts can be bought and sold by anyone, and the records of most of the trusts show that they are most in demand when the stock market is high – that is, when the units themselves, the shares on which they are based, are expensive – and least so when the market is depressed and shares are cheap. Managers of unit trusts can attest to the fact that the advertisements they place in the financial pages of the newspapers draw a more sluggish response when the markets are down than when they are up.

What is the practical answer to this sort of pattern of personal investment? If the fund managers knew, they would have devised a solution. As it is, the nearest that most have come to breaking out of the understandable but expensive habit of buying at the top is the organization of savings schemes, sometimes coupled with life insurance, so that each month the small investor puts something into stocks and shares, usually through a unit trust. It is not as exciting as playing the market, but it does mean that over time the investor will buy some cheap shares when the market is down as well as more expensive ones when it is up.

Of course, what every saver and investor wants to know is when the market is going to turn, when interest rates are going to shift and what is the best investment before the change takes place. One of the most important factors to watch for in this respect is, indeed, the movement in interest rates. In general, when interest rates fall share prices rise. This is partly because for the investor the value of the dividend paid on a share is greater than the fixed interest on a sum of money that is paid by the banker when that fixed rate falls, and partly because a fall in interest rates helps industry by reducing the actual costs of business and by encouraging sales, especially if those are on credit. So the clever investor who has put his money into a bank or a building society will start to move out when interest rates fall. The *really* clever investor will start buying shares just as interest rates are turning and should then enjoy the ride all the way up.

A safer but less exciting procedure is to invest in stocks with fixed interest rates, like gilt-edged British Government stocks, which also respond to interest-rate changes and, bought when interest rates are high, will not only produce a guaranteed income at the level that prevailed when they were bought but will also, if interest rates then fall, rise in value so that the investor can make a capital gain as well. But, as in all investment judgements, the safer course is also likely to be less dramatic, the upward swings (and the falls) smaller, than in the market for equity shares.

It is a truism that security and opportunity for big profits tend to be at the opposite ends of the see-saw. And this law applies not just to the sorts of investment and savings scheme that are on offer to the public; many another economic decision tends to follow this principle of caution and can therefore affect the whole economy as well as the individual.

There is really no such thing as *Homo economicus*, the imaginary being who (having read this book) weighs up all advantages and disadvantages before taking economic decisions. There is nearly always an element of what the chocolate manufacturers call 'impulse snack buying' (which means buying a chocolate bar at a railway station or newsagents whether you need it or not.)

A good example of this is the way in which people behave when prices start to rise. A sharp burst of inflation is very often accompanied by a rise in the savings rate; that is, just when money is becoming less valuable, people switch to holding more, not less, of it. It makes little economic sense because the extra money that they are holding will, when the time comes, buy less than it would buy if it were spent now. *Homo economicus* would save less (indeed, would go into debt) when he saw inflation accelerating, judging that he would find it easier to repay debts in the future, when money has fallen further in value. Perhaps he would use the debt to buy things like pictures, antiques, wine (for laying down, not drinking) or another house, things which would hold their intrinsic value as money fell, so that when he actually needed the money to buy food, to pay his bills, to educate his children or whatever, he could sell at a price higher than the one at which he bought.

If everyone behaved like that when inflation stepped up its pace, the savings ratio would fall in times of rising inflation. But on the whole it does not. Again, the reason is probably psychological, not practical. It seems that as prices rise sharply, consumers quickly notice the effect on shopping bills. They then make efforts to 'put more aside' simply in order to feel confident that if bills go on rising, they will have something in reserve with which to pay them. Holidays may be curtailed; buying the next new car may be postponed for a year; other economies may be made not because the increase in prices has put them beyond reach but because the householder is determined to save for the very rainy day which the rise in inflation seems to be bringing nearer.

There is, of course, another practical reason for this. When inflation begins to move more rapidly, both prices and wages tend to accelerate. On the whole, wages have kept pace with prices in most industrialized countries throughout the inflationary period of the last decades. But that is not how it appears to the average householder. The reason for a persistent sense that prices are rising faster than incomes is partly the demonstrable fall in the value of money, so that for all goods the hapless customer hands over more and more pound notes, and partly the fact that, in relation to family income, prices are rising faster for ten or eleven months of the year.

Where there is one breadwinner in the house there will be, by and large, one pay rise a year; where both spouses work, two. So domestic budget revisions upwards can come only when the *pay rises* start flowing into the bank, though the *price rises* are spread evenly over the whole year. According to the official figures, when your union has won a cost-of-living increase for you you may be just as rich the day after the pay rise as you were a year ago. Another way of looking at it is that the day before any pay rise you are just as poor as you were the day before the last one.

These factors loom much less large when inflation is moving slowly, and indeed the urgency of personal decision about money is reduced when money itself is holding relatively stable. When interest rates are down to 2 and 3 per cent, the chopping and changing and the careful investment calculations become much less important for the ordinary individual. Come to think of it, the great boom in financial and economic information which started when the daily and Sunday newspapers launched great City pages and business sections – a

boom from which I benefited as one of the early joiners of the
newly expanded crowd of financial journalists – coincided
almost precisely with the take-off of inflation, and therefore of
uncertainty about money and investment, in the early 1960s.

If I was a beneficiary of the new uncertainty – since more
financial journalists were deemed necessary and I was one of
them – for most people the uncertainty raised a whole host of
new problems. People suddenly had to make decisions between,
say, taking a holiday or putting the money in the building
society, for an entirely new set of reasons. If, for instance, there
was a chance that hire purchase terms might be eased, then a
holiday abroad might be cheaper next year than this, and in the
meanwhile the money that was not spent would be earning
interest in the building society or bank.

Judgements were not always easy. For a good while in the
late 1960s and early 1970s it was thought that an Englishman's
home was not only his castle but also his pot of gold at the end
of the rainbow. It was certainly true for so many years that it
became an established part of the accepted wisdom that house
prices would always rise so as to enrich house buyers by
comparison with tenants, whether in subsidized council housing
or in private rented accommodation.

This conviction rested on two factors, which are still in play
and worth observing. The first is that house purchase on credit
(through a building society or a bank) represents, for many
people, their largest single capital investment. The terms on
which money is lent for this very large investment are favourable: there is tax relief on the interest paid and no capital gains
tax on selling a house which has gone up in money value (as
long as it is the only one). The second, and enormously
important, reason for buying a house is that it is metaphoric-
ally, as well as literally, 'bricks and mortar'. Unlike savings
kept in money, which may fall in value fast (as described at the
start of chapter 5), or investments in stocks and shares, where
the chance of gain is usually matched by the risk of loss or
stagnation, a house is a house is a house. Understandably, in
view of the way property and house prices have moved in the

post-war years, the presumption that the private individual's largest single investment – his house – is also his best has persisted. But there is a catch.

To be sure, the *money value* of domestic property rises, subject almost exclusively to fashion and fortune in the neighbourhood in which the house exists. (Thus in an area of local depression house prices will fall, for the obvious reason that people tend to try and leave, rather than to move into, such areas.) But the *purchasing power* of the value of a house hardly rises at all. It is only if the owner, now turned seller, wants to buy something other than housing that his rooftree is worth a great deal. A friend of mine once sold two houses (one recently inherited) in order to buy an exceptionally well equipped round-the-world yacht for his family of four and, with what was left over, a smaller house to replace the two he had sold. This was a clear case of 'cashing in' the accumulated wealth represented by the houses. But if he had wanted to stay at home and house his family rather than sail round the world, the proceeds from selling the houses would not have bought him residential space on a scale equivalent to that of two houses. An Englishman's house is his pot of gold only if he is prepared to exchange it for a caravan!

Seen in that light, house purchase becomes a much more delicate business, and consumers should consider more carefully the precise terms offered in the house-buying market. That is why, for instance, there is always pressure on government to increase the nominal sum of a mortgage loan on the interest of which tax relief is given to the borrower.

Ingenious brokers and salesmen devise insurance policies and other schemes to make home-buying more attractive, but these do not necessarily simplify the decisions that individuals have to make. The range of choice is greater, the judgement no easier. One thing only is certain: a slowing down of inflation, if it lasts for a number of years and can be seen to have done so, will make the decisions of individuals far easier to make. Knowing where a family budget stands depends not only on secure employment – an area of uncertainty during a recession that is discussed in the next chapter – but also on confidence about the future value of money.

I have devoted some pages to the big decision for the house-hold, buying a house, but the same considerations apply at a more modest level to the motor car, kitchen equipment and, these days, the video recorder and second television.

Individual decisions about whether or not to buy will be swayed by the national economic climate, the rate of interest on hire purchase or the prospect for the next pay rise expected in the family budget. They will also, of course, have an immense impact on the national economy. It is one of the perpetual headaches of the highest in the land – politicians, or industrialists, or trade union leaders anxious for the security of the jobs of their members – that the consumer keeps on going out and buying a foreign transistor, or car, or calculator, or washing machine, or typewriter.

From the consumer's point of view, one of the easiest deci-sions to make is what to buy. Each individual has his or her own conception of value for money, and taste or convenience will play their proper part. It is more difficult to assess the financial niceties. And that is where the mass of information available to anyone who wants it should come in.

First, there are the newspaper columns. Most newspapers make an attempt to explain and amplify the choices available to readers when it comes to borrowing, insurance, investment and the rest of the range of financial services. For the quick of hearing, with poised pencil and paper, there is a handful of radio and television programmes that offer financial advice. And, of course, there are dozens of books. It is irritating that on the whole these services tend to serve least well those members of the public who need them most. The student of money will probably absorb information from a number of sources and will find it all quite helpful when he has to make a decision. For the far greater number, to whom the whole subject is mys-terious and vaguely threatening, the very considerable amount of advice on making the best of things that is available is literally inaudible or invisible because unheard or unread. For those who want to find out more about the financial environment in which they live and make their choices, there is plenty of opportunity, but the question of choice remains, including choice about which advice to follow.

Finally, in this chapter on personal finance and the sorts of decision that people try to make there is the question of motive. I was once asked – in my capacity as a financial journalist – to advise a most distinguished public person, a true VIP, to solve a quandry in which he found himself. Among the many voluntary tasks he undertook, Lord Hill of Luton, once the Radio Doctor, Charles Hill, and sometime Chairman of the BBC, was to address the Luton Savers Circle. It was at a time when inflation threatened to devalue the worth of savings certificates, perhaps by more than the rate of interest paid on them. To put money into National Savings might be to see its value eroded, actually to throw some of it away. On the other hand, the Luton Savers Circle was part of the National Savings Movement, devoted to the ideals of thrift, good housekeeping and putting something away for a rainy day. To advise the members not to save their money but to spend it while it still retained its value would have been contrary to the spirit of the occasion and of the movement. To extol too highly the virtues of savings certificates might be to gloss over the fact that they might not cover the future ravages of inflation. So we arrived at motive.

If the motive of the saver is to defer present consumption in favour of consumption at a later date, perhaps even by another person (a child, say, or a grandchild), then by all means he should save. If his motive is to maximize the value of the money concerned, then the question becomes more complicated. Its 'best value' may be realized by not deferring present consumption at all; the highest return may also be the riskiest. At least savings certificates are safe and will be repaid at face value.

Somewhere between the two may lie the proper course, and as well as the flood of information on every financial page and the advertisements competing with one another for the investor's cash, there is everyone from the bank manager to the expensive consultant to help the individual. So I end this chapter where I began it, with the thought that anyone wishing to move away from mere humanity to the mythical power of *Homo economicus*, who never gets it wrong, had better get hold of the mountains of books, magazines and financial pages and then decide whether to start reading or to run the central heating boiler off them.

# 18

# The Recession and
# the Individual

Although this book is intended to be an objective guide to making sense of the economy, equally useful in good or bad times, I cannot possibly ignore the present economic recession and its impact on the individual. The present levels of unemployment, not just in Britain but throughout the industrial world, are the highest ever experienced since the Great Depression of the 1930s and seem, according to many economists, likely to persist as far ahead as the forecasters care to look. This depressing forecast rests on three assumptions about economic life in the 1980s.

The first is that the very large increases in incomes and prosperity of the post-war decades are not likely to be matched in coming years. Growth rates of 6 per cent a year in Western Europe, almost casually achieved in the 1960s, now seem unattainble in the forseeable future. (The 'zero growth', 'small is beautiful' lobbies of the 1970s may see much to please them in this, but with it comes a heavy burden of unemployment.)

Secondly, the arrival of modern technologies in factories means that fewer hands will be needed to perform the same tasks in future. As we saw earlier, in Britain in 1981–2 'productivity' was rising far faster than output, and the inexorable consequence was higher unemployment.

Thirdly, there is the rise of newly industrializing countries. It is a safe bet that over the next few decades these countries, Korea, Taiwan and many another, will modernize along the lines already demonstrated by Japan, Hong Kong and Singapore and will compete fiercely for the markets into which the older industrial countries have sold their goods in the past. Thus there will be even more willing hands to produce the world's goods and continued pressure on employment in the older economies of the West.

What can the individual do about this predicament? In a sense, the individual is powerless to bring about the changes in society as a whole which may be needed to adapt to persistent high unemployment. He cannot alone bring about the sorts of change (like a shorter working week) that were discussed in chapter 3. Over time the older industrial nations will adapt to the fall in the need for industrial manpower, but in the meanwhile action remains with the individual. To some extent, the best guide to coping with the effects of recession is to see what has been happening in the past.

One discernible strand is that people have been 'trading downwards' in the labour market. That is, young entrants into the labour force have been prepared to accept less rewarding jobs than they would have sought ten years ago. Another aspect of the same strategy is the number of families in which both adults work. At first this may seem like contributing to the problem by increasing the labour force. But on closer examination it can be seen that in many cases a wife who takes on a part-time job to produce a second income is responding to a reduction in the earning power of her husband as, for instance, overtime is reduced in his trade or, quite simply, his 'real' earnings fall. In this case the couple are in effect work-sharing, each taking less than either would expect to earn in full-time, prosperous employment.

Shifts of this sort are not, of course, going to be available to everyone, although almost everyone is affected by the recession one way or another. Each individual is a consumer, a worker, an investor or all three, and in each of these roles his activities is affected by the general economic climate.

Take consumption first. On the whole we have done pretty well during the recession. There has been no rapid drop in the standards of living of average households. As already mentioned, the big impact on living standards has been felt by those who have been made redundant by the slump; for the rest, living standards, measured by 'real personal disposable income' (that is, income after allowing for both the rise in prices and tax changes), have risen for most of the time during the worst of the economic blizzard.

Any average is misleading because almost no individual fits the description. Almost without exception, each of us does better or worse than average. In the last few years, and especially at the start of the recession, the people who have done least well have been those most affected by inflation. As consumers, the people who have suffered most are those who started least well-off, simply because when the margin above essentials is very tight, any erosion by higher prices is noticeable. So throughout the period the number of people below the 'poverty line' has grown. But the persistent fact remains that *overall* personal consumption has not fallen. There have been some shifts in the patterns of living of consumers – perhaps fewer foreign holidays (or so the travel trade has reflected, as operators who have gone out of business testify). As mentioned in chapter 17, there was some sign that people increased their savings during the periods of sharpest inflation, and the savings ratio had risen to high levels by the early 1980s. The savings ratio, is the percentage of income which people chose not to spend on consumption. It is an uncertain guide, since 'savings' are calculated not by adding up all the money in savings banks, building societies and the like but by adding up all the income in the country and subtracting all the consumption: what is left must be 'savings'. In recent years the ratio has run at between 10 and 15 per cent, rising as high as 16.5 per cent in the second half of 1980, immediately after the peak in inflation of that summer, and falling back to 11.5 in 1982, both as inflation slowed down, some commentators assumed, as people *did* dig into their savings – or reduced the amount set aside each month – as in one way or another the recession affected their lives.

For consumers another salient feature of the later years of

the recession has been precisely the fall in inflation just referred to, though it has not been evenly spread. While inflation was still running in double figures at the start of 1982, the difference between different categories was staggering: for instance, in the twelve months to January 1982 the average prices of clothing, shoes and consumer durables like kitchen equipment and furniture did not rise at all. At the same time, rents, rates, charges for the services of nationalized industry services and taxation (on things like petrol and drink) were all on the up and up. From this it emerges that the individual as a consumer has to some extent benefited from the fruits of recession as prices rose less fast and people have been able to maintain their living standards.

But not everyone. For working people there has been a growing change in their circumstances. Even those who have kept their jobs throughout the recession have found the economic climate changing around them in a number of ways. Perhaps most evident has been the change in attitudes towards wage-bargaining. The very large number of well publicized occasions on which rank-and-file trade unionists have not pressed for strike action to improve a pay offer, even when offered the chance by their leaders, is the visible sign of literally millions of personal decisions to accept smaller pay increases.

As explained in chapter 6, a very important element in wage-bargaining is 'comparability', 'keeping up with the Joneses'. During the recession this ambition may have been blunted, so that even within one industry the workers at British Leyland in the very early 1980s accepted without demur wage settlements which were a good deal less than those being reached at Ford. Here the salient factor was that redundancy loomed larger at Leyland than at the more successful Ford, and the workers and their trade union organizers could see almost precisely how much less far they could push for more money, given the heavy losses in their part of a contracting industry.

Recession evidently sharpens the wage debate. Wage-bargainers in the 1981–2 wage round, for instance, had on many occasions to abandon the criterion formally established under the 'social contract' of 1974, which laid down that each annual pay award must fully compensate the work force for the loss of purchasing power of its wages since the last increase. On numerous occasions groups of workers settled for a good deal less than the rate of inflation current at the time of bargaining. (Because of the very rapid fall in the annual rate of inflation during 1982, many who had settled for less than the going rate of inflation earlier in the year found that quite soon the pace of price increases had fallen below the increase they had been given, and their hardship was mitigated.)

In general, in times of very high unemployment wage-earners become more conscious of forces other than simply the desire to catch up with inflation or to keep up with other groups of workers. The most important of these are the market forces which mean, when the going gets tough, that the price of earning too much and of demanding money-wage rates which are more than the economy can afford may not be just more unemployment in general: it may be the loss of one's own job.

At such times great efforts are made to spread work. The trouble, from the individual's point of view, is that work-sharing is very difficult to organize. The impetus must usually come from management, from the people who actually organize the work that is to be done. The figures show that before actually sacking people industry at large will tend to reduce over-time and to use short-time working in order to reduce labour costs when its output is contracting. But it has been difficult so far to organize on any large scale job-sharing schemes that are likely to be successful because they are also money-sharing schemes and that do not, therefore, throw an extra burden of cost on to the business just when it cannot be afforded.

If the lot of the worker is noticeably worsened in recession (as compared with what might have been, though not neces-sarily in absolute terms), opportunities for investment and initiative are also constrained. There will always be plenty of stories of people doing well in the worst of times. The sheer number of the new businesses that started up even in the depth of the recession suggests that some, at least, will prosper. But the hard facts of life are that bankruptcies and failures increase sharply in recession, and that for the individual as investor it is a time of higher than normal risk, even if there are countervailing influences. One of the hallmarks of the present recession has been the persistence of high interest rates for much of the time. So it has been relatively easy for anyone with spare cash to secure from that capital an income which has risen faster or run higher than the rate of inflation. And for those with money invested in the stock market there was the phenomenon in late 1982 and early 1983 of shares (as measured by the FT Index) rising to their highest values ever, even as, from the point of view of employment, the recession was continuing to deepen.

But stock market profits and the capacity to live off interest rates are the privileges of the few. For most people the preoccupation of the recession is to hang on to a secure job or, if by chance one job has been among the millions to go, to find another. This is by no means easy. Employment is often concentrated in certain areas of the country, for instance – though to a very real extent confidence even in normally reliable local industry may be misplaced. Local trade may appear to be the most dependable, and by tradition families serve the same industry for generations, but, as the steel and coal-mining communities of south Wales and the north-east recognize, the apparent security of a long-standing and traditional industry may be wholly illusory.

So, what is the aspirant to a secure job to do, in practical terms? Evidently not everyone who is seeking a job – whether school-leaver or mature worker made redundant in mid-working life – can discover a new job in a secure and prosperous industry. However, the job seeker can make use of a number of helpful indicators which are to be found even in the depths of a recession.

If his or her family is fortunate enough to see the problem coming some way off – that is, if it recognizes, while a future job seeker is still at school, that getting a first job may be more difficult than automatic – then there are a number of things to do. The first is to pay attention to the ordinary news of the economy – at least to try by following the sorts of developments discussed in this book, to spot the 'losers' ahead. In general, these may be the older industries in which job security has already been seen to be tenuous.

And the past must be a guide of some sort. What has been happening in the past fifteen years or so in the industrial west has been a move away, in terms of employment, from heavy traditional manufacturing industry to other forms of employment. Many of the new jobs are in service trades, and much is made of the new wave of opportunities in 'information technology'. So if the job seeker is quick enough off the mark, research into what skills are needed for these trades and crafts can be a major help.

The individual is not entirely on his or her own in this business of optimizing job prospects. One thing that distinguishes the current recession from that of the 1930s is the early recognition by Government that the problem of unemployment is one which requires official concern with individuals as well as the general welfare net of unemployment benefit and other social services support. As a result, there are now a very large number of schemes to help people either to find work or to occupy themselves with training or further education. This book is not intended as a guide to these schemes; and in any case, if it attempted the task, it would certainly become out of date very quickly, as the various provisions for training and 'job creation' are refined and developed quickly. So the rule of thumb is to track down the local offices of the major agencies: the Manpower Services Commission, the Department of Health and Social Security, the Department of Employment and the relevant local authority. Between them these have responsibility for training, for job opportunity schemes, for adult education schemes (the lcoal authority) and, if the worst comes to the worse, social security payments.

The state and local government picture is only half of the whole, for even though the public sector has grown so large, it is still smaller, in terms of employment than the private sector of commerce, industry and business. In the private sector too the consequences of recession have been drastic, but while the total labour force of industry has contracted in the last few years, it is still recruiting.

In many trades employers are trying to save money by reducing or eliminating apprenticeship schemes, but certain truths remain in spite of the recession. The competitor in the job market needs the best hand of cards possible. This means qualifications, of course, though these need not always be of the most obvious kind. One of the best publicans I know qualified as a motor mechanic, with a three-year apprenticeship, and filled in the gaps raising broiler fowls from day-old chicks on a chicken farm and doing jobbing gardening.

In a sense, coping with the recession is bound to be an individual problem. The individual has, however, a number of options. First, he can become resigned: a recent newspaper article, noting that a very small proportion of those registered for unemployment benefit are also applying for work at their local Jobcentres, suggests that this may be happening in some places. Second, he may be more assertive and use the various public amenities, from Jobcentres and training to job-creation schemes, local or national. Third, he may (and by saying 'he' all the time I don't exclude 'her' – she may be on the look-out too) bring all available energy to bear and tackle the private sector. This means, of course, using local newspaper advertisements but also going further – nagging local trade associations and even contacting chambers of commerce and business to find out (if only to be disappointed) which employers in the neighbourhood or elsewhere run privately the sorts of public schemes run by government or, plain and simple, which have vacancies.

When all is said and done, being unemployed is both a financial and a personal deprivation. But there are other things an unsuccessful job hunter can consider: self-employment, for example, or voluntary work (in the latter case a certain proportion of expenses can be re-claimed without jeopardizing the worker's already difficult financial position.) And while we are on that subject, it should not pass without comment that the financial position of the unemployed is nothing like as disastrous as it was before the war. Not only has unemployment benefit been increased in line with the cost of living, but the other benefits of life under the umbrella of the welfare state, however meagre, deliver the unemployed from the worst of the Depression blight into which their parents might have fallen. The opening of an unemployment benefit office in a Spanish holiday resort a few years ago provoked shrieks of derision and cries of 'Costa del Dole' from the sprightlier tabloid newspapers, but it stands as a symbol of the fact that a redundant workman may now draw his due under Mediterranean sun, whereas before the 1970s he would have been entitled to draw it, during his holiday, only from another British benefit office.

Trade union organizations may also be a help to their own members, but it has to be said that they do not always give the appearance of total co-operation. After a recent plant closure in the motor industry two skilled workers applied for jobs at a neighbouring factory where their abilities could have been used in jobs which had been advertised, without success, for some weeks. The works manager was pleased to get two well qualified men to fill his long-open vacancies – until he heard from the trade union which held sway in his factory, as in the one which had been closed, that the two men could not be taken on. It turned out that because, confronted with a total plant closure, the men had accepted redundancy pay, their union construed this a 'voluntary' redundancy and enforced a ruling of its own executive that no one who had accepted the redundancy money should be admitted into any closed shop run by that union for at least one year – even if no one else at all applied for the job.

Against this sort of ruling the individual has little recourse, and for hundreds of thousands of workers who have lost their jobs in industry the search for new occupation has been a long one. Many may, in the end, never return to normal, full-time working. In the early 1980s a good deal was made, however, of the potential of the 'black economy'. Here, it was thought, where jobs were done for cash and no one was any the wiser, there might actually be a vast number of 'employed' people who were dropping out of the statistics but nevertheless doing, in the immortal phrase of Damon Runyon, 'as best they can'. Common sense suggested that the out-of-work would turn their hands to odd-jobbing and that the 'black economy' could be providing a fair number of people with an alternative to normal, wage-earning employment. It is true that quite a number of men who had been laid off in industry attempted to get together in small groups to carry on, at their own initiative, where conventional employment had left off. However, mostly these ventures were not in the 'black economy' but in the conventional, tax-paying side of life. The British Steel Corporation (BSC), for instance, has had some success with a scheme which has helped thousands of redundant steelworkers in hundreds of enterprises – most of them very small – to start up new businesses, with BSC providing the expertise and showing the men where to go for official aid, grants and the like.

Another branch line from the dole queues was the attempts by a number of groups to foster co-operatives in which the workers would band together to run their own businesses. I call it a branch line because although there were some successes, the total numbers involved were very small by comparison with the flood tide of redundancies in industry as a whole.

And the same, it seems, may be true of the 'black economy'. In the later 1970s and early 1980s several studies were made of the phenomenon. Many people assumed that because there was more interest in this cash-payment, non-taxpaying slice of society, it must be growing during the recession. But, equally, it has been suggested that in fact the 'black economy' has suffered as much as anyone else and that hard times have hit moonlighters and part-timers as much as they have affected the regular merchants and traders.

It is an area – not surprisingly – about which little precise information is available, though the Inland Revenue does make periodic estimates of how much tax it is 'losing' by virtue of the 'black economy'. What seems certain, however, is that if there has been any increase in the size of the 'black economy', like the co-operatives it has made only a very small dent in the total level of unemployment.

# 19

# The Taxman Cometh

This is a true story. In the mid-1960s my father, Roy Harrod, the Oxford economist, was invited to teach for a term (or semester, as they say) at the University of Pennsylvania in Philadelphia. As he made his preparations, a colleague told him that he would need to pay no income tax, either in the USA or in Britain, on the generous payments he would receive as a visiting professor because of the cultural exchange provisions of the Double Taxation Relief Treaty then in force between Britain and the United States. He immediately sought expert opinion, first from his bank manager, then from an accountant. Both seemed surprised that an eminent economist should be making such an inquiry. They supposed that if he did not disclose the payment to the Inland Revenue, there was no reason to expect officials to find out. Irritated both by the imputation that he might be seeking to cheat and by their lack of knowledge, he grasped the nettle firmly and approached his tax inspector. 'Of course, Sir Roy,' the inspector said, 'That will be perfectly in order.'

I include this story not only for its own sake – the charm of virtue rewarded even in the lion's den – but to make the point that taxation can be a co-operative as well as a combative affair. Systems of taxation are indeed often set up or modified by Governments in order to win the co-operation of the public or of industry in some social, political or economic venture. On a tiny scale the cultural provision of that Double Taxation Treaty with the USA is one; on a much larger scale was the Selective Employment Tax (SET) enacted by the 1966 Labour Government, which was designed to encourage employment in manufacturing industry, rather than the service trades, by means of a rebate to manufacturers on the tax levied on all employers according to the numbers that they employed.

SET got a bad name and was later repealed by the Conservatives. But just before its demise a study was published which showed that far from increasing prices in the service sectors on which it bore, the tax had actually tended to reduce prices. The findings of the study revealed that in the retail trade the impact of the tax had persuaded employers to manage their businesses with fewer staff. It was believed to have given a strong impetus to the movement, already underway, towards self-service, the supermarket and more economical shopping. That is only one example, though a vivid one, of the way in which the tax structure influences decision-taking, from industry to the individual.

The basic structure of British taxation is simple enough – taxes on income, capital and expenditure – though VAT, which is the main instrument of the latter objective, is a complicated vehicle. But even given this fairly simple structure, there are considerable arguments about how taxes actually work.

On the face of it, income tax redistributes income from the rich to the poor, in the sense that the poor tend to derive more absolute benefit from the services provided out of government spending funded by income tax, in any case pay less tax and are therefore relatively better off than the rich who pay more tax. But VAT and excise duties (on drink, tobacco, motoring), the taxes on expenditure, tend to do the reverse. The rich can afford to spend a smaller proportion of their income on the current consumption on which these taxes are levied than can the poor, a larger share of whose income therefore ends up in the taxman's net.

Taxes on capital – capital gains tax, the capital transfer tax which replaced death duties – evidently penalize the better off, who have capital gains to be taxed and riches to pass on to each other, but the yield of capital taxes is not large enough, in the overall picture, to qualify as a redistributive tax.

These social effects, the almost casual concomitants of the real purpose of taxation – to raise revenue for the Government – are nonetheless the focus of much of the argument about tax.

'Progressive' income tax is favoured by socialist theory, since it bears most heavily on the rich, even though the higher rate bands (in one memorable year increased to over 100 per cent by Roy Jenkins, as Chancellor of the Exchequer, in order to raise a capital levy on the very richest) are more punitive than redistributive, since they, like capital taxes, produce precious little revenue. Conservative Governments have argued that lower taxes on income will increase personal incentive, and even though in the inflationary early 1980s the Government found it very difficult to lower the total burden of income tax, the top rates were sharply reduced, in the interests of incentive, in its first major Budget.

While disagreeing about the shape of income tax, politicians on both sides have recently favoured shifting the burden of taxation from taxes on income to taxes on spending. This seems to be partly because spending money is deemed less virtuous than saving or investing it in the future of the economy, and partly for the down-to-earth reason that in other countries income taxes are lower, expenditure taxes higher.

At the heart of the debate about how to tax is the question: how do people react to being taxed? Back in chapter 1 we considered the Chancellor of the Exchequer's Budget judgement, one important element of which was the 'stimulus' given to the economy by cutting taxes. It is virtually axiomatic that if taxes are cut, people will spend some of the extra money they have got on consumption, and the real economy will receive the stimulus intended to increase output.

Seen from the other end of the telescope, from the position of the taxpayer, how does it work? One thing which seems absolutely certain is that although no Government has chosen to say so, a cut in income tax has, for the taxpayer, precisely the same effect as a pay rise. It does, after all, turn up in just the same way – as more money in the weekly pay packet or a larger monthly pay cheque – once the Government's decision has been translated into action. Equally, an increase in personal income tax (or National Insurance contributions) has the same effect as a reduction in pay.

What is less certain is the effect on spending of changes in taxes, VAT or excise duties on smoking, drinking or driving. It is difficult for individuals to react swiftly to such changes: you cannot quickly change habits like using a car on business in response to higher petrol tax. All that can be said is that changes in tax provide the rough and ready 'regulator' which is designed to influence individual behaviour and in general does so. But before moving on to some possibilities for tax reform of a fundamental kind, a couple of examples of unsought effects of tax changes.

The first I have already mentioned: the impact of the virtual doubling of VAT in Britain to 15 per cent in 1979. This, the Prime Minister was advised, would have a short-term effect, lasting three or four months, and would add perhaps 3p in the pound to the actual cost of living. That calculation, in good faith, ignored the crucial fact that the increase in prices would remain a potent bargaining counter in wage negotiations, and not just for a few months but for the whole year ahead. Along with other factors, the VAT increase contributed to a climate in which average money earnings were pushed up at such a pace that claims reached 22 per cent a year twelve months after the Budget that had introduced the higher tax.

Another example of untoward results from a tax change dates back a good deal further. In the late 1960s the American President, Lyndon Johnson, announced his intention to ask the American Congress for a 10 per cent surcharge on income tax to help pay for the USA's war spending in Vietnam. In the USA tax changes are not just announced; they are argued over among the politicians for months on end. On this occasion every twist of the argument was reported in the newspapers and elsewhere under such headlines as '10 per cent tax hike debated' and so on. In fact, what was contemplated was an increase of income tax which would take about 1 per cent out of the pay packet (being a surcharge of 10 per cent on *tax*

*already paid*, not on 10 per cent of income.) The confusion of
the American taxpayers was so complete that during the
period before the tax came into force people started saving
more of their wages against the harsh times ahead. When the
dread day arrived and pay packets were docked by only 1 per
cent, the relief was so great that the taxpayers all relaxed,
started spending more money, not less, and quite upset the
American Government's economic strategy.

These sorts of complexity and misunderstanding are among
the reasons why tax reform and simplification is always in the
air. Still on the sidelines, but potentially interesting, are two
contenders for tax reform: negative income tax, or variants of
it, and expenditure tax.

The first of these is an old favourite for those who want to
simplify the tax system, and it would work by providing, for
any family with an income below a certain level, a single
benefit or credit which would make up the basic family
income. Anyone with more income than the limit would start
paying tax. The system would have the merit of administrative
simplicity; it would be possible to scrap all the numerous
present allowances, benefits and means-tested payments which
can be claimed by the less well-off but quite often are not. The
difficulty about negative income tax lies in setting it up. At
what level to you establish the family income limit? How
should it be varied between single persons, married couples,
those with children, one-parent families?

So far the most active work on something like a negative
income tax has been undertaken by the Social Democratic
Party (SDP) as part of its potential programme. But the SDP
has gone only as far as to concentrate on the replacement of the
married couple's allowance with a larger child credit scheme.
(The replacement of child allowance by a cash child credit
was a first small step in the same direction.) At the moment
discussion of the scheme still revolves around ways of redis-
tributing the tax burden as between families and single people
and so on. The issue of the removal of all payments like
National Insurance and all benefits like family incomes supple-

ment into one single scale, which would range from support at one end to higher rates of income tax at the other, has been ducked, though a complete replacement of the present complex system with the simplified version would eventually save a good deal of administrative time and costs.

The second reform, suggested a year or so ago by Dr James Meade and the Insititute for Fiscal Studies, is even more radical. Based on income, expenditure tax would work like this. In each year's tax return the taxpayer would include a statement showing by how much his total savings and investments had risen or fallen during the year. If he had spent less than he had earned (if his savings had gone up) he would be taxed *only* on what he had spent. If he had spent more than he had earned (if his savings had fallen) he would be taxed not only on all of his income but also on his extra spending out of savings. Tax on income would rise only when income was spent on consumption, not when it was put towards savings or investment.

The realization of these ideas for the reform of the present personal tax system is still a long way off. For the moment most decision-taking energies are devoted to assessing how to minimize tax liability without trespassing into the territory of tax evasion (illegal) from tax avoidance (legal). As might be expected, this is a little industry in itself, and one of its major manifestations is reckoned to be the 'black economy'. The decision to pay or be paid in cash is not, of course, illegal: even a Chairman of the Board of Inland Revenue recently admitted to the practice in his own household dealings. The line of illegality is crossed only when the recipient hides the payment from the Inland Revenue.

But even then, I ask myself, where is the borderline between and illegal 'black' payment to a gardener or window cleaner, if that gardener or window cleaner is my teenage son or next-door neighbour? And what of the element of the housekeeping money that goes not on food or the maintenance of the house but on a blouse, a pair of tights or, in the bad old days before my wife gave up, a packet of cigarettes? Isn't that part of the monthly housekeeping cheque actually *pay*? Before agonizing too much over whether my wife should declare that part of her allowance to the income tax authorities, I console myself with the thought that in any case it would be far too small a sum to exceed her personal tax allowance.

# 20

# Conclusion

One of the finest views in London is from an office on the fifteenth floor of the Vickers building, on Millbank, in Westminster. Directly below, winding its way eastward, is the Thames. It is flanked on the left by stately buildings (but not very tall ones): the Electricity Council offices, the Department of Energy, the ICI building, now being sold but nonetheless imposing. Of these only the roofs, air vents and lift machinery can be seen.

The first building of any distinction, and far enough away to be seen as a whole, is the Palace of Westminster, from the Victoria Tower to Big Ben, from the House of Lords to the House of Commons. Then farther off, the discerning eye can pick out the architecture of Whitehall, the sweep of the river under its bridges and, in the distance, the dome of St Paul's Cathedral and the tower blocks of the offices of the great financial centre, the City of London itself.

To the right the south bank of the river is less grand, but there is Lambeth Palace, seat of the Archbishop of Canterbury, and, if the eye is raised a trifle, a glimpse of the railway lines running into Waterloo Station. Apart from being a magnificent view on a fine day, it comprehends the nerve centre of the economic modern world: Parliament, the Civil Service, the City and commerce.

Turn your back on the plate-glass window, step from the spacious office through a modest lobby and you enter a board-room. On one day a month the view here is no less comprehensive, for we are in the offices of the National Economic Development Council.

For more than fifteen years, on and off, I have been taking the lift up to this floor to hear a post-mortem on the monthly meeting of the NEDC, or 'Neddy'.

Around the circular table sit about twenty people: there are Ministers of the Crown, usually led by the Chancellor of the Exchequer, though once a year or so he will cede his seat as Chairman to the Prime Minister; there are six members of the TUC Economic Committee, led by the General Secretary; there are the leading lights of the CBI; there are independent members representing such various interests as the Consumer Council and the Bank of England, which shows its respect for this montly meeting by being represented by the Governor. It is, you might say, economic decision-taking made visible.

While it is an economic forum, Neddy can talk about more or less anything. I have heard reports of meetings touching on lower fuel prices for industry, on the desirability of allowing skilled workers to jump council house lists (if they move to a new area to find a job and fill a vacancy) and on the suggestion that trade unionists and businessmen should be nominated to serve on secondary-school governing bodies to urge for more teaching that is related to industry and work.

Neddy has two distinguishing characteristics. First, founded in 1962 by a Conservative Chancellor of the Exchequer, Selwyn Lloyd, it has been successively nurtured and strengthened by Governments of both major political parties. Secondly, there is an unspoken rule that however awful the relations between the parties to Britain's economic debate, the Government, the TUC, the CBI, they will go on meeting at Neddy.

In the last two decades, however, the members of Neddy have been observing steady decline. At first, the decline was only relative. Britain was still doing well, and living standards were rising, perhaps not as fast as those of other European countries and more distant nations but, of course, with a good deal further to catch up. Latterly, the decline has been absolute. As chronicled in earlier chapters, output has fallen, unemployment has risen and for many people absolute living standards have stopped going up. Worse, if the economists are to be believed, the prospects for recovery are slim and the chances that any recovery will return Britain or the industrial West to the path of growing prosperity enjoyed for twenty-five years after the war remote or nonexistent.

This book has tried to look at the economy as an organism which can be studied – and without the apparatus of technical knowledge or mathematics. What are the conclusions?

Right at the start, considering the choices facing the Government at the annual Budget, the complexity of the scene became apparent. With so many different influences to cope with, it is not surprising that Governments do not always find it possible to steer the economy towards the steadily rising prosperity that they would like to deliver to an expectant electorate. Uncertainties even among professional forecasters, some of whom advise the Government, do not help. But it is the real world, not that of the forecasters, that counts, the world where industrial output is measured and where the number out of work, counted monthly, begins to shed light on the predicament of the economy.

And though those figures have provided a gloomy background for most of the recent meetings of Neddy in London, it is obviously not just among the wise men around the table on the fifteenth floor of the Vickers building that decisions are taken which may influence the state of the economy. The staff who support this monthly meeting and produce the working papers which initiate the debates on economic affairs also support a network of less exalted, but perhaps more important, groups around the country. These are the 'little Neddies', or Economic Development Committees, for various parts of industry and the country. Then there are the sector working parties set up in the 1970s as places where the decision-takers of industry and their trade union counterparts meet to thrash out the problems of business, commerce and industrial relations.

Out of the 'little Neddies' pours the information which will go to help countless decisions in Manchester, Glasgow, Liverpool or Leicester. And back through the network will come the complaints – and occasionally the success stories – of the numerous firms up and down the country whose provincial bases are the sources of business and profit. For most industrial managers and trade union organizers London is a remote place, whence come political decisions to change their tax regime or their terms of employment and where the general national debate on the economy is decided. For them the priority is their own immediate patch: keeping things going at the factory and making ends meet. Their wider horizons include the whole world, not just the political and Civil Service centres, for they will be looking for sales wherever they are to be found. Often the discussion, if not the decision-making process, takes place in the industrial centres, not at the political hub. The meeting described in chapter 12, at which the trade union and management teams in the British tyre industry met, was in Birmingham, close to many of the plants where the problem it faced was to be resolved by investment or by closure. This confronting of the future of falling employment in tyres was, as a matter of fact, organized through a sector working party whose staff office is within the Neddy organization.

It should not be forgotton that the people around that table in the Vickers building are also representatives of that most important group, the final buyers ('consumers', as they appear in this book.) As I have said, it is not practical to describe precisely how consumers behave, especially in the uncertain economic climate of the last quarter of the twentieth century. Although everything, in the end, depends on what consumers want and what they can afford, they seem to be affected equally by the uncertainties of inflation and of unemployment, which loom most clearly as the problems of the future. All economic decision-takers, mighty and humble, want to escape the joint evils of unemployment and rising prices, the predicament of the early 1980s.

That predicament, some think, can be resolved by the stringent application of the rules of 'sound money', though the argument persists about whether the amount of money available affects prosperity or simply inflation. But it is unquestionable that inflation – or the loss of purchasing power – has been the most dramatic change on the economic canvas in the last twenty years or so. It has led to, or has been fuelled by, the great wages chase. Thirty years ago wage increases were awarded only for seniority or merit. Now as money goes down wages go up, and the volatility is compounded by feuding over 'comparability', relative pay and the government's role in incomes policies.

While the paperchase over money and wages goes on, so does the march of progress. And this means that higher output from every worker is a reality even as the worldwide recession deepens and the number out of work increases. The recession of the 1980s colours everything, not least the growing concern about public expenditure, about the ever-increasing share it takes of national output and the consequences of that for the major economic decisions which have to be faced by Government. And the debate continues about how we should run our local government – and pay for its services – and whether the state should administer so much else through nationalized industries and the state monopolies.

It is in this environment that the world of business and commerce has to go about its affairs, testing the confidence of investors on the stock market, worrying about the level of trade, trying to make decisions about new investments – let alone coping with the hundred and one decisions, faced every day in every company boardroom and at every branch office and factory, over production, design, marketing and industrial relations.

As if that were not enough, the pattern of international trade is undergoing change at a time when expansion and prosperity no longer seem just around the corner. The uncertainties of foreign trade and payments have been vastly greater since 1971 and the collapse of the post-war monetary system. Closer to home there is the great political and economic enterprise of the EEC, flawed but probably still the most important attempt at economic co-operation now running in the West.

None of these issues is neglected at that round table on the fifteenth floor of the Millbank Tower where the wise men of

Neddy hold their monthly meetings. Some of them, like some of us, are reluctant to try to hold every strand of the fabric of the debate in their hands. One man wants the best for his members; another wants to make sure his profit margins are high enough to provide for the investment that will let him keep his business going; a banker is concerned that the value of money should not keep wasting away; a Minister, dexterous in argument, defending a line, has perhaps to fend off his regular companions in this eyrie over the Thames.

They have all made their appearances in the last twenty chapters, cast in their proper roles as decision-takers, great or small. They are the people who shape our world, but perhaps, for all of their eminence, they have as much trouble as we in making sense of the economy.

# PART IV

# An Economic Calendar

# An Economic Calendar

Making sense of the economy requires, above all, facts and figures. Most of the figures used by politicians, economists and laymen alike are the official statistics published by the Government or by independent bodies like the CBI or the Society of Motor Manufacturers and Traders. In the calendar which follows some of the raw material from which economists work is set out. First there are the regular monthly series, then the quarterly figures, then the occasional publications.

But the student of economic affairs needs to follow the deliberations of decision-takers as well as the results of their efforts that are reflected in the statistics, so the calendar also includes a schedule of the most important regular meetings at which the economy is the meat of the agenda and a handful of bulletins, reviews and the like which may lead the reader on to the closer scrutiny of the economy towards which this volume has been offered as a first, small step.

| Event | Source | Comment | Reference(s) |
|---|---|---|---|
| **Monthly figures** | | | |
| UK official reserves | Bank of England (second working day of month) | Figures showing Britain's holding of foreign currency for trade | Chapter 13 |
| Unemployment figures | Department of Employment (first or second Thursday of month) | Provisional figures showing unemployment and vacancies nationally and by region | Chapter 3 |
| Trade figures | Department of Trade | Figures for United Kingdom overseas trade (imports and exports) and estimates for 'invisible' trade in other services | Chapter 13 |
| Building societies | Building Societies' Association | Figures for deposits and withdrawals from building societies, which are very responsive to interest-rate changes and sometimes indicate likelihood of future changes in rates | Chapters 4, 17 |
| Housing starts and completions | Department of the Environment | Figures showing trends in house building | Chapter 10 |

| | | | |
|---|---|---|---|
| Wholesale prices | Department of Industry | Figures showing prices paid by industry for materials and fuel and prices charged by industry for goods leaving factory gate | Chapter 5 |
| Vehicle production | Department of Industry | Figures for car and lorry production; *see also* new car registrations, also monthly | Chapter 10 |
| Retail sales | Department of Trade | Figures for the value and the volume of retail sales, also divided into categories | Chapter 10 |
| Index of industrial production | Central Statistical Office | Measure of the output of industry, broken down into industrial categories | Chapter 3 |
| Central government borrowing | The Treasury | Figures showing extent of central government borrowing | Chapter 4 |
| Index of average earnings | Department of Employment | Figures showing both average earnings for all industries and basic wage rates; often used in comparison with prices to measure movements in living standards | Chapter 6 |

| Event | Source | Comment | Reference(s) |
|---|---|---|---|
| Retail price index<br>Tax and price index | Department of Employment<br>Central Statistical Office | The major measures of the rise in prices ('inflation') | Chapter 5 |
| Hire purchase figures | Department of Trade | Figures showing new and outstanding hire purchase debt | Chapter 3 |
| *Industrial Trends Survey* | Confederation of British Industry | The CBI compiles a brief monthly trends survey and economic comment, as well as a fuller quarterly survey in January, April, July and October | Chapter 3 |
| **Quarterly figures**<br>Consumers' expenditure | Central Statistical Office | Estimates of consumers' expenditure, used in economic models and for forecasts | Chapter 2 |
| PSBR | Central Statistical Office | Quarterly estimates of total PSBR, including local authority borrowing | Chapters 4, 8, 12 |

| Indicator | Source | Description | Reference |
|---|---|---|---|
| Manufacturers' stocks | Department of Industry | Changes in stocks and work in progress in industry; an important guide to manufacturing activity | Chapters 2, 10 |
| Capital investment | Department of Industry | Figures for investment by industry in new factory building, machinery and equipment; a very important guide to prospective economic progress or decline | Chapter 11 |
| GDP/GNP | Central Statistical Office | The national income measured by Government once a quarter to give the overall view of the economy; measured by reference to total output, total spending and total income | Chapter 3 |
| Real personal disposable income | Central Statistical Office | Personal income, after allowing for taxation and for rising prices, to give an estimate of the buying power of family income; the simple measure of living standards | Chapter 6 |

| Event | Source | Comment | Reference(s) |
|---|---|---|---|
| **Occasional figures** | | | |
| The Budget | The Chancellor of the Exchequer | As well as incorporating tax changes, the Budget presented to the House of Commons in March or April offers an economic review of the year and a sketchy and tentative forecast for the future *see also* FSBR below | Chapter 1 |
| FSBR | The Chief Secretary to the Treasury | The *Financial Statement and Budget Report* published on Budget Day sets out the detail of the Government's forecasts for the economy and the effects of Budget changes | Chapters 1, 2 |
| Autumn statement | The Chancellor of the Exchequer | A statement to the House including some 'mini-Budget' changes and outlining the Government's current forecasts | Chapter 2 |
| Public spending | The Treasury | A White Paper on public spending by central and | Chapter 8 |

| | | | |
|---|---|---|---|
| | | local government published once a year (now January, but movable; *see also* PESC below) | Chapters 1, 8 |
| PESC | Government Departments | In midsummer the Government's own review of future spending gets under way; figures 'leak' from official sources and through occasional speeches | Chapter 1 |
| Debate on the Finance Bill | House of Commons | A few weeks after the Budget the Finance Bill, embodying its changes, is introduced and debated in the House of Commons, allowing opportunity for changes and for more detail of economic policy from Government benches | Chapter 1 |
| Treasury Select Committee | House of Commons | An all-party Select Committee of the House of Commons discusses Treasury and Civil Service affairs and issues occasional reports; there is also a Committee on Public Spending | Chapter 1 |

| Event | Source | Comment | Reference(s) |
|---|---|---|---|
| **Reviews** | | | |
| Bank of England Quarterly Bulletin | Bank of England | The quarterly review charts the progress of the economy with articles and with detailed financial statistics, March, June, September, December | Chapter 2 |
| Economic Progress Report | HM Treasury | A monthly short review published by the Treasury with articles of topical interest on economic policy and management | Chapter 2 |
| National Institute Economic Review | National Institute for Economic and Social Research | The National Institute publishes a quarterly Economic Review with articles of topical interest, an updated forecast and statistical tables | Chapter 2 |
| CEPG | Cambridge University Department of Economics | The Cambridge Economic Policy Group publishes one of a number of forecasts from university sources and | Chapter 2 |

| | | | |
|---|---|---|---|
| London Business School | London Business School | has a reputation for strong writing and accurate prediction | Chapter 2 |
| Miscellaneous | | Another regular forecast with a high reputation | |
| | | A number of stockbroking firms in the city of London publish monthly forecasts or newsletters | |
| OECD *Economic Outlook* | Organization for Economic Co-operation and Development, Paris | Twice a year, in July and December, the OECD publishes *Economic Outlook* for the two dozen or so richest non-Communist countries which make up its membership. The outlook provides prediction and analysis but tries to avoid too much policy prescription. (The OECD also publishes, once a year, a review of the British economy, as of the economies of each of its member countries) | Chapter 13 |

| Event | Source | Comment | Reference(s) |
|---|---|---|---|
| **Statistics**<br>*Economic Trends* | Central Statistical Office | The invaluable monthly publication of official Government statistics, including charts as well as tables to illustrate the course of the economy. (Most of the national statistics listed in this Calendar are published in *Economic Trends*.) Published by the Stationary Office; available in reference libraries | |
| *Monthly Digest of Statistics*<br>*Financial Statistics* | Central Statistical Office | The *Monthly Digest of Statistics* and *Financial Statistics*, also monthly, contain fuller tables than *Economic Trends*, giving a running service of all the major economic statistics available | |

*International Financial Statistics*

International Monetary Fund, Washington, DC

*International Financial Statistics*, published monthly by the IMF in Washington, gives the major indicators of economic performance, including foreign trade, interest rates, wages, etc., for the more than 140 countries which are members of the IMF and includes rich and poor countries, only excluding members of the Soviet bloc

**Meetings**
NEDC

National Economic Development Council

Monthly meeting of TUC, CBI and Government Ministers on economic topics; the major tripartite forum on the UK economy

Chapter 20

| Event | Source | Comment | Reference(s) |
|-------|--------|---------|--------------|
| TUC | Trades Union Congress | The TUC is the bureaucracy of the trade union movement, providing a secretariat and committees for the trade unions affiliated to the central body. Monthly meetings include those of the General Council – the decision-taking body – and the Economic and the Finance and General Purposes Committees of the General Council, which meet at Congress House in London. The decisions taken by the General Council are supposed to be based on the decisions of the annual Congress, which is held in the autumn at a seaside resort | |

CBI    Confederation of
British Industry

The CBI holds meetings of
its Grand Council once a
month attended by members
drawn from the management
of private manufacturing,
nationalized and other
industries. It also holds
frequent regional meetings,
and an annual conference,
to whose decisions in debate
the officials and Secretariat
of the CBI in London are
supposed to be subject

OECD    Organization for
Economic Co-operation
and Development

The OECD in Paris holds
frequent meetings of officials
from member countries on a
number of committees
considering aspects of
international economics;
there is a meeting at
ministerial level in the
summer

| Event | Source | Comment | Reference(s) |
|---|---|---|---|
| IMF/World Bank | International Monetary Fund & World Bank Group | The largest single gathering every year – in late September or early October – of the Finance Ministers and many of the private bankers from the non-Soviet Communist world. (China, though Communist, is a member.) The meeting hears speeches about economic co-operation, national policies and, notably, development problems facing the poorer nations | |
| Industrial summits | Summit secretariat | For the past few years the seven richest industrial countries (Britain, Canada, France, Germany, Italy, Japan and the United States) have arranged summit meetings of their heads of Government (Prime Ministers or Presidents) | |

with Finance and Foreign Ministers; they are intended to co-ordinate the economic policies of the West and happen about once a year, in rotation among the seven members

EEC

Member countries of the European Economic Community

There are regular meetings of the Ministers of the member countries of the EEC to discuss economic and diplomatic affairs. This body (or bodies, for Ministers attend according to subject) is the Council of the EEC. (There might be a Fisheries Council on fishing or a Budget Council on the Community Budget.) There are also, twice a year, meetings of the European Council, which is a summit meeting of heads of Government of the Community members

| Event | Source | Comment | Reference(s) |
|---|---|---|---|
| BIS | Bank for International Settlements | The Bank for International Settlements is a pre-war institution which acts as a bank among its member countries; the members of the board, which meets once a month, are the heads of the central banks of the member countries (W. Europe, North America, Japan); important only in crises, otherwise, very discreet | Chapter 13 |

# Index